Cliffe*Hangers*

The Most Common Questions Asked of Campus Evangelist Cliffe Knechtle

CHRISTIAN SANELLI

Cliffe-Hangers: The Most Common Questions Asked of Campus Evangelist Cliffe Knechtle

Cliffe-Hangers: The Most Common Questions Asked of Campus Evangelist Cliffe Knechtle, Copyright 2016

To Julian and Kaitlyn, my children, who I hope will grow up to have deep faith and a passion for apologetics as well, but much more the former.

To Julis, their mother, who has shown great love to me in my darkest times, and who clings to her faith even in the most miserable and despairing of situations.

Table of Contents

1 Introduction 9

2 Cliffe's Background 13

The Questions 17
   3 Are Morals Absolute? 19
   4 Does God Exist? 23
   5 Is Jesus Christ God? 45
   6 Is Hell Just? 51
   7 Why Is There So Much Pain and Suffering? 59
   8 What's Wrong With Sex? 69
   9 Do We Have Free Will? 73
   10 Creation Or Evolution? 77
   11 Is The Bible True? 81

12 Other Open-Air Preachers 85

13 Miscellaneous 91

14 Why I Wrote This Book 97

Appendices
   A: Cliffe's Books 101
   B: Give Me An Answer Television Program 103
   C: Cliffe's Online Debates 105
   D: Some Campuses Which Cliffe Regularly Visits 107
   E: Student Organizations Sponsoring Cliffe 113

1

Introduction

"I … do … not … know", admits the outdoor evangelist with the booming voice, while with one hand he points to the fingers on his other as he slowly and deliberately says each word. Confronted by a challenging question on Christianity, long-time open-air campus evangelist Cliffe Knechtle is not too proud nor embarrassed to admit when he doesn't have the answer.

I first saw Cliffe in October 1991 as a graduate student at the University of Illinois at Urbana-Champaign. Cliffe would step out on the U of I quad each day, around noon, when students were walking around en masse to travel to their next class. He would stand near a busy sidewalk and begin with a short, 2 or 3-minute story with a Christian message. With his natural booming voice that made one mistakenly think he was speaking through a microphone, Cliffe would begin to attract a small crowd. After his short monologue, Cliffe would open the discussion up to questions or comments, often by saying something like "That's all that I have. Now I'd like to open it up for comments and questions, agreements and disagreements, wherever you all are coming from". Thus began a 3 to 5-hour back-and-forth with the student body on questions ranging from atheism to miracles to homosexuality to alleged Biblical errors to women's role in the Church to Hinduism to any of a wide range of issues on the minds of the mostly-undergraduate group encircling Cliffe. Most of the questioners were polite and honest seekers of truth. A few were deliberately contentious, attempting to stump or belittle Cliffe any way they could.

I picture Cliffe's open-air theological arguments with the gathered public to be reminiscent of what took place in first-century Palestine, where theological debate was commonplace. I am very pleased that Cliffe continues this tradition 2,000 years later. Cliffe is an intelligent man and deeply committed to Jesus Christ and His commission to believers to "Go into all the world and preach the gospel to all creation"[1]. He thoroughly enjoys visiting college campuses every year and engaging students in thoughtful, reasoned discussion and debate on the veracity of Christianity.

I grew up in the 70s in a predominantly Italian-American suburb of Rochester, New York. I was raised Roman Catholic. Being of Italian ancestry, most of the people in my neighborhood were Roman Catholic as well. This meant that, although we owned a bible or two, it wasn't a book we read very much. However, when I arrived in central Illinois in my twenties in 1991 to pursue a PhD in mathematics at the great University of Illinois at Urbana-Champaign, it was a bit of a culture shock to see a predominantly Christian, but non-Catholic, presence on campus.

One week during my first year at the U of I, the famous college evangelist Josh McDowell spoke in the evenings at a lecture hall on one end of the sprawling U of I quad. I don't recall what the topic was about, but it was very well-attended and extremely interesting. It was perhaps my first introduction to the world of Christian apologetics. Later that year, in October 1991, Cliffe Knechtle showed up as a guest of Illinois's chapter of InterVarsity Christian Fellowship (IVCF), the largest Christian student organization on campus,

---

[1] Mark 16:15, NIV.

and I was told the second-largest IVCF chapter in the United States. I was probably informed about Cliffe's arrival from a friend at the time, Mark Ashton, who was on staff then at IVCF, and is now a senior pastor of a large community church in Omaha.

That first year I was at the U of I, I was not a Christian in the orthodox, saved, born-again, true sense of the word. I was still a practicing Catholic who felt was in a land of Protestants who rashly discarded the "one, true Church" in the 1500s, and who were now flailing around theologically as a result of their initial Reformation-era errors. But, somewhat frequently, I would be approached on campus by an evangelical student who would shock me with frank questions such as "If you were to die tonight, would you go to heaven?" or "Do you know Jesus Christ as your personal Lord and Savior?" And, every fall, during the week before classes began, the U of I held their annual Quad Day, a fun festival where most student organizations would set up a booth to introduce themselves to the large arriving group of new undergraduate and graduate students. It seemed that every third booth out of the 100+ booths was for a Christian organization or local church. One of them had a Velcro dartboard and challenged student passersby to try to hit the center of the board using a Velcro ball. The activity was likened to one trying to earn their way into heaven. If the student missed the exact bullseye, that meant they had sinned at least once in their life. Probably without exception, the student would miss the bullseye, which meant they were headed for hell. Then the Christian manning the booth would explain that Jesus died on the cross for their sins, and that if the student would just accept that payment for their sins, God would ignore the fact that they "missed the mark" and they would be welcomed into heaven once they died.

But one partly-sunny day on the U of I quad, in October 1992, when Cliffe was speaking, I became a Christian in the true, orthodox, biblical sense of the word. I remember the scene quite vividly. I was sitting on the grass with my legs crossed, backpack to my side. I was contemplating something which Cliffe had said. I was perhaps a few minutes into this reflection, with Cliffe likely talking then about something else, when I was overcome with a feeling of urgency. I became frighteningly aware that if I died that instant, or on my walk back later to my dorm room, that I faced a definite risk of consignment to an eternity in hell. I had become intimately aware of the Bad News behind the Good News of Jesus's saving sacrifice on the cross.

Preachers don't mention the Bad News as much as they do the Good News. But why is the Good News good? It is good precisely because it proclaims a way to escape the absolutely terrible Bad News which is that we "all have sinned and fall short of the glory of God"[2] and that we therefore deserve death[3]. Sitting on the quad that day in 1992, the Holy Spirit convicted me of my grave spiritual state and my immediate need for a Savior. I quickly put my hands together and prayed earnestly that Jesus would save me from having to go to hell. I asked Jesus if He would "take the reins" of my life and that "His will be done".

---

[2] Romans 3:23, NIV.
[3] Romans 6:23.

2

Cliffe's Background

Robert Cliffe Knechtle was born on Thursday, May 20[4], 1954, to Emilio Knechtle and Ann Johnston[5]. He was born in New Canaan, Connecticut, the town which he still calls home.

Cliffe follows in the footsteps of his father, who was an international evangelist and revivalist. Born in Switzerland in 1922, Emilio B. Knechtle emigrated to the United States in 1946. Raised Roman Catholic, he became a Seventh-Day Adventist and was described as a "spiritual giant in pointing thousands of people to Christ and His righteousness"[6]. He authored several books and was fluent in no less than five languages. He retired in 1990 and passed away in 2006 at age 83. Several audio versions of his sermons can still be found online.

---

[4] The same day of the year as another great American and practicing Christian, my favorite actor, Jimmy Stewart, from the Christmas classic 'It's A Wonderful Life'.

[5] Cliffe may have been born instead Christian Robert Cliffe Knechtle, according to http://www.geni.com/people/Christian-KNECHTLE/6000000004271447414, as accessed on September 14, 2013.

[6] http://archives.adventistreview.org/article/473/archives/issue-2006-1510/adventist-news

Cliffe is one of 6 children, 4 boys (Cliffe, David, John, and Stuart) and 2 girls (Grace and Heidi). One of them, his younger brother Stuart, attended Princeton University. I believe this is the brother which Cliffe frequently mentions as being a surgeon who performs kidney and liver transplants.

Cliffe got his first degree in 1976, in history, from Davidson College, a liberal arts college in Davidson, North Carolina. While there, he participated in InterVarsity Christian Fellowship. Six-foot-one-inch Knechtle was on the 1974-75 Davidson Wildcats basketball team. I found a stats sheet online with his performance. It was … well, Cliffe himself says he wasn't a great player - that he had a great seat for the game, watching it from the bench.

He got his second degree, a Master of Divinity, in 1979 from Gordon-Conwell Theological Seminary, an evangelical seminary centered in South Hamilton, Massachusetts. He seems to have not needed to write a thesis for this degree, as Gordon-Conwell has no record of one for him.

Beginning in 1979, he worked for InterVarsity Christian Fellowship as an evangelist in the Boston area. He is an ordained Southern Baptist minister and has been doing open-air evangelism since at least 1980.

He has 3 sons - Robert, Stuart, and Ian - and no daughters. His wife Sharon (nee McDonald) has worked fighting against sex trafficking worldwide. His son Rob has given the message at his church, and attends or has now graduated from his dad's alma mater, Gordon-Conwell Theological Seminary.

Regarding Cliffe's personal spiritual journey, it says in the April 15, 1983, Davidson College newspaper The Davidsonian:

'Knechtle says he didn't always believe in God. He had a conversion experience as a child. One day he walked down the stairs in loneliness and asked Jesus, "If you are the truth, I want to know." After that time he said he no longer walked alone.'

As for powerful spiritual influences in his life, besides his father, he was heavily influenced by Leighton Ford[7], an evangelist for 30 years with the Billy Graham Evangelistic Association.

Cliffe's TV program Give Me An Answer debuted in 1990 and, besides the United States, airs in England, Australia, New Zealand, and India. The content of these shows is the Q&A from campuses he visits during the year. For the last several years, his ministry has posted these programs on YouTube. He now has a dedicated YouTube channel, askcliffe (https://www.youtube.com/user/askcliffe), with hundreds of these programs, as well as many short Q&A clips and a few debate videos.

He has been the senior pastor of Grace Community Church in New Canaan, CT since 2001. Their website is gracecommunity.info. One can find many recordings of his sermons there.

---

[7] http://www.leightonfordministries.org

The Questions

Let's now look at some of the most common topics that Cliffe discusses in his responses to questions from students on college campuses.

3

Are Morals Absolute?

"In argument about moral problems, relativism is the first refuge of the scoundrel."
-- contemporary philosopher Roger Scruton

"Man is the measure of all things."
-- Protagoras, 5th century BC

Are morals relative to the individual? Are they relative to the culture? Does each of us decide what is right and what is wrong? Does a particular society decide what is right and what is wrong? If this is so, then anything can be deemed moral. Genocide, torture, rape, pedophilia, and so on - all is morally acceptable - indeed, all of this can even be considered morally good. Each of us can do what we wish, and no one else can rightly say that we are morally wrong.

Questions that relate to this idea, known as moral relativism, are without a doubt the most frequent queries Cliffe receives when visiting college campuses. Every time I've seen Cliffe speak, this topic came up so often that it was at times tiring. A lot of undergraduates believe that morals are relative to the individual or to the culture. Why do so many believe this? Several reasons are to blame. Perhaps foremost is the belief in modern Western society that people should not judge the beliefs of others. "To each his own" is the mantra. Cliffe points out that, since World War II, people have become accustomed to multiculturalism. If one culture buys into gassing Jews, then that's ok. If another culture buys into cannibalism, that's also ok – that's just their culture. People feel that it is arrogant for someone to claim a God-centered system of moral judgment. In a climate of political correctness, truth often gets trampled underfoot.

A more selfish reason some students ascribe to moral relativism is their inner aversion to submitting to the will of a higher authority. If there is no supreme being dictating morality, then they can be the arbiters of their own actions.

There is also often a suspicion of objective truth in academia. There is a tendency to not want to admit that something is absolutely, definitively, indubitably correct. One of the reasons for this is a healthy critical attitude toward claims until they are vetted and shown to be valid or not. But one of the reasons is not so noble. Often an air of political correctness or a fear of being challenged prevents the truth from being proclaimed as truth.

To highlight the hard-to-stomach consequences of adhering to a belief in moral relativism, Cliffe often brings up Adolf Hitler and his Nazi regime. He says that, while we might strongly believe that Hitler's extermination of six million Jews and millions of others was definitely wrong, it wasn't wrong in Hitler's eyes and that, unless you have an overarching authority which dictates morality, then what Hitler believed and carried out can not be considered objectively wrong. Cliffe mentions the Nuremberg war crimes trials of 1945 and 1946. He tells the story of how 24 Nazi officers were defended by a brilliant German defender who once brought the trials to a halt by exclaiming that his defendants were not at fault because they were raised in a culture where Jews were deemed inferior, and that they were just following orders when they exterminated them. But then the American attorney, Robert H. Jackson, argued that there is a higher moral authority than the authority of any country or regime, that of God, and that authority declares that killing for no other reason than the belief that a people is inferior or subhuman is morally abominable. The trials started back up and the Nazi officers will ultimately convicted of crimes against humanity.

Cliffe often uses a member of the audience to make the point against moral relativism. He looks at a student near him, says he can use his hand, roll it up into a fist, and smack the student, or he can use his hand to reach into his pocket and give the student some money to buy dinner with. He says it's entirely a matter of choice. And neither choice is objectively right or wrong in a world where morality is relative.

Cliffe is absolutely correct in attacking moral relativism. I've seen it online rightfully called "mind cancer". It is a self-refuting position, because if person A says "What you believe is right for you, and what I believe is right for me", person B can respond by saying that that statement itself is incorrect, meaning that what person A believes is right for himself is actually not. So moral relativism is shown in this way to be logically inconsistent.

This is one of the greatest flaws of atheism. Without a God, there is no objective moral compass. Words like 'should' and 'ought' lose their meaning. The world becomes a scary place where nothing is ultimately off limits.

Cliffe has students realize that living out that worldview, the worldview that says morality is relative, is impossible. Each and every day, we all make countless value judgments, "thou should not" judgments. So those who adhere to moral relativism are hypocritical in their daily lives. If they see an old lady being attacked and kicked in the street, to be consistent, they shouldn't be morally offended. They should be morally neutral about the attack, thinking "for the attacker, what he is doing is justified by his personal set of morals".

But this is absurd. We all (save for sociopaths and the intellectually challenged) understand this.

And yet, the case is not closed. Just because lack of belief in a God implies that there is no objective basis for morality, this does not necessarily imply that there must be a God. A lack of a universal law to call horrible actions what they are is indeed very unpalatable, but it does not mean that such a law must in fact exist. There are good points to be made that people have evolved to have a sense of morality, for the benefit of civilization as a whole. See, for example, atheist Michael Shermer's book The Science of Good and Evil[8].

---

[8]Michael Shermer, 'The Science of Good and Evil: Why People Cheat, Gossip, Care, Share, and Follow the Golden Rule', Times Books, 368 pp, 2004.

4

Does God Exist?

"Religion has actually convinced people that there's an invisible man, living in the sky, who watches everything you do every minute of every day of your life. And he has a list of ten things he does not want you to do. And if you do any, any, of these ten things, he has a special place full of fire and smoke and ash and torture where he will send you to suffer and burn and scream and cry forever and ever until the end of time! … But he loves you."
-- George Carlin (1937-2008), comedian

"In crossing a heath, suppose I pitched my foot against a stone, and were asked how the stone came to be there; I might possibly answer, that, for anything I knew to the contrary, it had lain there forever: nor would it perhaps be very easy to show the absurdity of this answer. But suppose I had found a watch upon the ground, and it should be inquired how the watch happened to be in that place; I should hardly think of the answer I had before given, that for anything I knew, the watch might have always been there. (...) There must have existed, at some time, and at some place or other, an artificer or artificers, who formed [the watch] for the purpose which we find it actually to answer; who comprehended its construction, and designed its use."
-- William Paley, Natural Theology (1802)

There is arguably no more important question asked of Cliffe, or asked by anyone of anyone, than the question "Does God exist?" It makes nearly all other questions pale in import. Mankind has pondered this question for millennia. It colors all of our lives – the way we think about ourselves, our behavior, others, the world, etc. It is the gnawing, overarching question at the heart of our existence.

Many students on the campuses Cliffe visits are not believers in the existence of God. Among these students there are four main groups:

GROUP 1:
Those That Are Certain That God Does Not Exist

These are what have been called hard atheists, positive atheists, or even militant atheists. They positively believe that there exists no God. This group comprises a very small percentage of all atheists.

These are the people Cliffe is referring to when he uses the term 'atheists'. But this is not the definition of an atheist that most modern atheists use. Those people constitute the next group.

GROUP 2:
Those That Just Don't Have A Belief In God's Existence, But Are Open To The Evidence

An atheist is usually meant to just mean one who does not have a belief in the existence of a God. He just lacks a belief in God. The Oxford English dictionary, considered by many to be the standard of the English language, says that an atheist is a "person who disbelieves or lacks belief in the existence of God or gods".

These students are the ones Cliffe is primarily aimed at reaching. If he can provide persuasive evidence for the truth of Christianity, then he hopes he will help save some of them from hell.

GROUP 3:
Those That Believe That Ascertaining Whether God Exists Or Not Is Impossible And Thus Futile

These are agnostics. They believe that the question of whether God exists or not is unknowable. These students may listen to Cliffe for a while, but tend to move on after a short time, since they believe it is just a waste of time discussing the evidence for or against the existence of God.

GROUP 4:
Those That Are Apathetic Toward God's Existence

There are also a number of students who don't have a belief in God, or at least an active belief in God, but are generally apathetic toward the question of His existence. This group sometimes manifests itself by heckling Cliffe as they walk by him on campus. One time at Ohio State University, Cliffe exhorted a heckling passerby by answering back that "God gave all of us two ends: one to sit on, and the other to think with. Our entire future depends upon which one we use. Heads you win, tails you use. You've got to use your brain and think. Think! God gave you that ability. It's a great gift. Use it well."

Why Cliffe Believes That God Exists

There are several reasons Cliffe gives for why he believes that God exists. In his Give Me An Answer YouTube video #1810[9], he lists out eleven:

1. The order and design of the universe point to an intelligent mind behind it

---

[9] Cliffe's YouTube campus videos are numbered with the format NNYY, where YY is the year in which the video was broadcast on his Connecticut TV program, and NN is the order of the video shown that year. It doesn't represent the year or order that the video was recorded.

2. The universe is not eternal, implying someone started it
3. The anthropic principle
4. The amount of information densely packed into DNA
5. Irreducible complexity
6. Moral absolutes
7. Love
8. Rational minds
9. Man's innate drive for meaning
10. Historical Resurrection of Jesus
11. Never seen life come from nonlife

Let us look at each of these reasons in turn. After this, at the end of the chapter, I will give some of my reasons why I believe God exists.

(1) The order and design of the universe point to an intelligent mind behind it

This is known as the teleological argument, or the "argument from design". It is a classic argument for the existence of God, and goes back at least to the great ancient Greek philosopher Socrates. There is amazing order and seeming design in the universe, from the structure of objects like galaxies, stars, and planets, down to the perhaps unfathomably complex structure of organisms such as insects, flowers, bacteria, and cells.

Take, for example, viruses. Even the tiniest of viruses have some 500,000 base pairs in their DNA. For people, there are over 3,000,000,000 base pairs. That amount of information, if written out one character to a nucleobase (G, A, T, or C), could fill perhaps 10,000 books.

Something that I am truly dumbfounded by is the sheer immensity of the universe. Take our galaxy, for example. The Milky Way galaxy has some 400 billion stars[10], most of which are larger than our own sun. Now consider that the universe has at least 100 billion galaxies. That means that there are at least 40,000,000,000,000,000,000,000, or 40 sextillion, stars in the universe. How many is this? Well, for each grain of sand on all the beaches on earth, there are roughly 10 stars in the universe[11]. Wow! The next time you are at a beach, pick up a handful of sand grains and marvel at how large a number 40 sextillion truly is.

Now consider the immense separation between stars in a galaxy. The nearest star to the Sun, Proxima Centauri, is over 4.2 light-years away. That's a distance of roughly 24,937,000,000,000 miles! If the distance from earth to the sun is represented as an inch, then Proxima Centauri would be over 4.2 miles away! Given this incredible distance, and given that there are 10 times more stars in the universe than grains of sand on the earth's beaches, we can now begin to understand just how nearly unimaginably enormous the universe truly is!

Another amazing thing in nature is the seeming design of the interplay between species. Consider the codependence of the bucket orchid and the orchid bee. From Wikipedia[12]:

> *Both depend on each other for reproduction. One to three flowers are borne on a pendant stem that comes from the base of the pseudobulbs. The flower secretes a fluid into the flower lip, which is shaped like a bucket. The male orchid bees (not the females) are attracted to the flower by a strong scent from aromatic oils, which they store in*

---

[10] Astronomy, December 2015, p. 23.
[11] http://io9.com/are-there-more-stars-than-grains-of-sand-on-the-earths-1471951896, accessed August 18, 2014.
[12] http://en.wikipedia.org/wiki/Coryanthes

*specialized spongy pouches inside their swollen hind legs, as they appear to use the scent in their courtship dances in order to attract females. The bees, trying to get the waxy substance containing the scent, sometimes fall to the fluid-filled bucket. As they are trying to escape, they find that there are some small knobs on which they can climb on, while the rest of the lip is lined with smooth, downward-pointing hairs, upon which their claws cannot find a grip. The knobs lead to a spout, but as the bee is trying to escape, the spout constricts. At that same moment, the small packets containing the pollen of the orchid get pressed against the **thorax** of the bee. However, the glue on the pollen packets does not set immediately, so the orchid keeps the bee trapped until the glue has set. Once the glue has set, the bee is let free and he can now dry his wings and fly off. His ordeal may have taken as long as forty-five minutes. Hopefully, the bee will go to another flower, where, if the flower is to be successful at reproducing, the bee falls once again into the bucket of the same species. This time the pollen packets get stuck to the **stigma** as the bee is escaping, and after a while the orchid will produce a **seed** pod.*

The bee, having stored the aromatic oils in his back legs, can then fly off to mate with a female bee.

Could this all be a product of evolutionary processes without an intelligent being behind it, or does it point to the workings of a supremely intelligent creator? Upon initial reflection to most people, it would seem to be the work of a superior mind. However, upon further reflection and scientific study, it can seem possible that there are alternate explanations that do not require the existence of the supernatural. See the later chapter 'Creation vs. Evolution'.

(2) The universe is not eternal, implying someone started it

Is the universe eternal, or did it begin at some point in the distant past? This is a hotly-debated question. Cliffe brings up a famous argument known as the Kalam Cosmological Argument. This argument was formulated in the 11th century by the Islamic theologian and philosopher Al-Ghazali. The argument can be posed simply as:

(1) Everything that had a beginning had a cause
(2) The universe had a beginning
(3) Therefore, the universe had a cause

He then says, since nothing cannot cause something, the cause of the universe must be God.

The Kalam Cosmological Argument (KCA) is perhaps most often associated with my favorite Christian apologist, the great William Lane Craig. Dr. Craig wrote his doctoral thesis on the argument[13] and refers to it in nearly all his numerous formal public debates.

The argument is clearly valid, since the conclusion (3) necessarily follows from the premises (1) and (2). The debate is whether the argument is sound. Opponents of the KCA attack each of the premises, most often the second one. They propose that, even if the Big Bang began our universe, this universe is just one of an infinite series of universes, without beginning or end. This is known as the multiverse theory.

There are other KCA opponents who rebut the first premise. One thing that is said is that by "everything that had a beginning had a cause", we mean of course that everything that had a beginning IN TIME had a cause. But, since time is understood to have "begun" itself at the Big Bang, then the beginning of the universe was not an event "in time". Consider this analogy. If someone were to ask you to think of one person older than you, we could probably all think of one person readily. And if we happen to be quite old, say in

---

[13] http://www.reasonablefaith.org/double-doctorates

our 90s, we might not personally know of someone older, but we could go online and easily find someone who is older. So it would be easy to assume from this exercise, if we didn't know better, that **everyone** could think of someone older than himself or herself. But this of course would be a false assumption. There is always one person on earth who couldn't think of, or find, no matter how hard he or she tried, someone older. This person is, of course, by definition, the world's oldest person. Similarly, it could be considered a false assumption that everything that had a beginning had a cause. This analogy, like most analogies, has its problems, but it illustrates nonetheless that premise (1) is not a certainty.

(3) The anthropic principle

There are several physical values in our universe which, if altered ever so slightly, would mean that we, and all other life, would not exist. In many cases it would even mean that galaxies, stars, and planets would not exist. For example, if the strength of gravity were different than it is by just 1 part in 10^100, the universe wouldn't be life-permitting, according to physicist P.C.W. Davies.[14]

Cliffe has brought up the distance of the Earth to the Sun. It is roughly 93 million miles. Cliffe says that if the Earth was much closer to the Sun, then we'd all fry. If it was much further, then we'd all freeze. There are many more cosmological constants for which if each of them varied by just an infinitesimal amount, then our universe would not be life-permitting.

This seems to be powerful evidence for the existence of a creative intelligence that set these parameters carefully so that

---

[14] The Accidental Universe, 1982, p. 107.

the universe would produce life and, in particular, us. But there is fervent argumentation that the fine-tuning is either not so finely tuned or that theories such as multiverse theories, which propose that ours is just one of several (or even an infinitude of) universes, render the fine-tuning probabilities not as amazing.

(4) The amount of information densely packed into DNA

The human genome consists of roughly 3 billion base pairs. There are 4 unique base pairs in DNA. Each person inherits two sets of genomes, one from their mother and one from their father, for a total of 6 billion base pairs.

How much computer media storage does this represent? Each unique base pair can be represented by 2 bits, because 2 binary bits can hold $2*2 = 4$ distinct values. So a byte, which has 8 bits, can hold the value of $8/2 = 4$ base pairs. So 6 billion base pairs can be stored in 1.5 billion bytes, which is about 1.4 gigabytes. This is roughly the storage space of 2 compact discs. This is a large amount of data packed into one tiny DNA molecule.

(5) Irreducible complexity

Irreducible complexity is the concept that certain biological systems are just too complex and inter-connected to have possibly evolved from simpler systems via natural selection. The concept is linked with Lehigh University biochemistry professor Michael Behe and his 1996 book "Darwin's Black Box". In that book, Behe offers the mousetrap as an example of a system which is irreducibly complex. A spring-loaded bar mousetrap has five interacting parts: the base, the catch, the spring, the hammer, and the hold-down bar. Remove any one of these five pieces and the mousetrap does not function as intended.

Behe's point is that evolution doesn't account for systems such as this - that these systems could not have been formed by successive, slight modifications. With respect to the mousetrap, Behe argues that you don't have a viable system with only four of the five parts. But Dr. John McDonald disagrees and wrote a rebuttal paper.[15]

Dr. Behe also brings up the bacterial flagellum, an appendage which allows many bacteria to move. Behe claims this is a good example of irreducible complexity. Another would be the human eye with its complex set of interdependent parts.

Charles Darwin wrote of the potential power of irreducible complexity to destroy his theory by writing that "if it could be demonstrated that any complex organ existed, which could not possibly have been formed by numerous, successive, slight modifications, my theory would absolutely break down."[16]

Although on first thought irreducible complexity sounds persuasive, there are many strong critiques of its claims and logic.[17] For example, systems missing a piece or two, while not perhaps working in the same way as the full system, might still be functional.

(6) Moral absolutes

See the prior chapter on moral relativism.

---

[15] http://udel.edu/~mcdonald/mousetrap.html
[16] Charles Darwin, Origin of Species, 1st edition, p. 189.
[17] http://www.talkdesign.org/faqs/icdmyst/ICDmyst.html

(7) Love

Cliffe believes that mankind's innate ability to care for his fellow man is evidence for the existence of God. I certainly see his point here. If there was no God, why would we be caring creatures? Why would we care about the well-being of others, especially strangers? Why would Mother Teresa sacrifice her life to help the plight of the poor and diseased in India?

There are some atheists who argue that people innately care for their fellow man due to purely evolutionary reasons. One of them is Michael Shermer. See again his book 'The Science of Good and Evil'[18].

(8) Rational minds

If God does not exist, how is it that blind evolution has resulted in rational minds from the irrational, from a mindless "blind" evolutionary process?

Cliffe mentions a letter written by Charles Darwin to a Mr. Graham wherein Darwin is disturbed with an issue which arises from the realization that man may be genetically related to apes. Darwin writes:

"But then with me the horrid doubt always arises whether the convictions of man's mind, which has been developed from the mind of the lower animals, are of any value or at all trustworthy. Would any one trust in the convictions of a monkey's mind, if there are any convictions in such a mind?"[19]

---

[18]Michael Shermer, 'The Science of Good and Evil: Why People Cheat, Gossip, Care, Share, and Follow the Golden Rule', Times Books, 368 pp, 2004.

(9) Man's innate drive for meaning

We seem to have a deep hunger to determine why we are here – why we exist, individually and collectively. We feel that there must be a greater purpose for our life, more than just to eat, sleep, work to put food on the table, find a mate and procreate, then get old and die, to decay and become basically nothing. If that is all there is to life, then how are we substantially any different than the animals or even more primitive life forms?

And if there is no real meaning to our life, no transcendent meaning, then why should we go on living? Cliffe refers to the 20th-century French atheist Albert Camus, who said that the only important question for a man to answer is whether or not he should commit suicide. To Camus, life was clearly absurd. The realization of this absurdity of life without a higher purpose leads many atheists to despair as the chief reaction to life.

(10) Historical Resurrection of Jesus

This is obviously a major reason to believe in God's existence. In fact, all of Christianity rests or falls on whether Jesus Christ actually died and rose again on the third day. Paul affirms this when he writes "if Christ has not been raised, our preaching is useless and so is your faith".[20]

Cliffe points to several nearly-universally attested-to facts: that Jesus really died, that He was buried in the tomb of

---

[19] Charles Darwin letter to W. Graham, July 3, 1881.
[20] From 1 Corinthians 15:14, NIV.

Joseph of Arimathea, that His followers dispersed in despair and disillusionment, and that beginning three days later, He appeared risen from the dead over a period of 40 days to over 500 people in different places and at different times.

(11) Never seen life come from nonlife

Do we have an example of when we've seen in a laboratory life come from nonlife? We do not. Nothing animate has ever been witnessed to come from the inanimate.

Another argument Cliffe brings to bear is known as the Moral Argument. People generally have a conscience, a "moral compass" as Cliffe often puts it, which tells us what is inherently right and what is inherently wrong. He asks where this conscience originates from if not from God. Generally all people without physical issues have this innate sense of right and wrong, unless they've committed enough acts against their conscience to sear it.

There are many well-known proponents of the idea that morality comes from God, from the great philosopher Immanuel Kant to Cardinal John Henry Newman to more recent Christian giants like C. S. Lewis.

There are those however who believe that even our conscience is an evolutionary byproduct. One of the newer examples of these is one of the "Four Horsemen of the New Atheism", Sam Harris. He propounds this view in his 2011 book The Moral Landscape.

Summary of Cliffe's reasons

These nearly dozen reasons for believing in God's existence given by Cliffe are powerful reasons. I urge the reader to meditate on them, and pursue further study where desired.

Some students seem to want certainty that God exists. Cliffe retorts by saying that we can't live our life demanding total certainty. He points out that the student doesn't have certainty that his roommate won't stab him in the back that night while he's sleeping, and yet he still has a roommate and goes to sleep without that fear.

Cliffe also says "You don't know if your mother, when she has you over for Thanksgiving dinner, won't drop arsenic in your food." And yet you trust her because of a lifelong loving relationship with her where you know that she wants your best and does not wish to do you harm.

Disturbing admission

Nonetheless, despite Cliffe's firm belief in the existence of God, he does admit that he may be wrong. He has admitted during his campus visits that God may not actually exist.

Extraordinary claims and evidence

There is a popular mantra that goes "Extraordinary claims require extraordinary evidence". Many people believe the great 18th-century philosopher David Hume was the source for this quote, but it was actually 20th-century American sociology professor Marcello Truzzi who first said "Extraordinary claims require extraordinary proof", and then the late great cosmologist and author Carl Sagan popularized it as "Extraordinary claims require extraordinary evidence".

It is a claim that I believe is entirely valid. If someone were to tell you that there is a platypus living in a zoo somewhere, how much evidence would you need to believe this? Not much. You can google 'zoos' and 'platypus' just to be sure. This is all the evidence you would need. Now, if someone were to say however that there was a pink, polka-dotted platypus living at a zoo somewhere, you would need more evidence. You would want to see a picture of it online, and make sure that that picture wasn't a joke. You might even want to visit that zoo to see this freaky platypus for yourself.

Now let's say that someone claimed there was a 10-mile-wide, pink polka-dotted platypus living in the Andromeda Galaxy. NOW what kind of evidence would you need? Would you just take this person at their word?

My take

I have studied apologetics for over 20 years now. During this time, I've amassed a sizable collection of books on apologetics and theology, attended several Christian-atheist debates, been to several apologetics conferences, listened to perhaps over 100 debates, watched many live online talks and debates, read magazines and books, had countless deep discussions with pastors and theology-interested friends, and a host of other things. My chief goal in this huge investment of time and money has been to discover the truth about life, God, and my role and responsibilities, if any. I wish I could say I've been rewarded with many answers to life's biggest questions, but if I did that would be a lie. I have a lot of knowledge now about the Bible, philosophy, and apologetics, but I have far from certainty on the reality of things supernatural.

But I've slowly come to believe that this is the way God wants it. God doesn't want us to "prove" that He exists. He doesn't want us to reduce Him to logical arguments. He wants us to "lean not on [our] own understanding"[21]. He wants us to have faith. Even Cliffe has said "there's no way that you'll ever intellectually work your way to God"[22]. Likewise, French mathematician and philosopher Blaise Pascal wrote in the 17th century:

> *"Let us say: 'Either God is or he is not.' But to which view shall we be inclined? Reason cannot decide this question.'*

I do have some faith. Sometimes – oftentimes - it is very weak. Sometimes it feels that I have no faith at all. Many days I feel that there likely is no God. I often feel sad and bitter that my investment in searching for the truth seems to have paid off so miserably. Yet I have also experienced some incredible events and moments, things that I can not and will not write off to coincidence.

My faith is also buttressed by incredible people I have known, even if briefly, and true stories that I am aware of. Let me tell you about some of them.

When I was a graduate student at the University of Illinois, one weekend evening in 1991 I was walking with a friend toward campustown, eager to enter a bar or dance club so I could see some attractive undergraduate girls and perhaps, against the usual course of events, meet one or two of them and perhaps hit it off. Approaching the first corner of

---

[21] Proverbs 3:5.
[22] Faithful Witness: The Urbana 84 Compendium, IVP, edited by James McLeish, 1985, p.23.

campustown, there was an elderly gentleman, perhaps 75 years of age, who stood out easily as most everyone else around was 25 or younger. He was passing out tiny copies of the Gospel of John to students as they were eagerly headed to the bars, and I'll never forget what he said each time he handed one to a student: "More valuable than gold!" I never saw this man again, but I'll never forget that comment of his, nor the peaceful joy I saw in his face.

Another person I won't forget is a Catholic priest I met in Florida in 1999. I had gone to some Christian theology weekend about an hour north of Tampa, where I was living at the time. At one point during a break in the day's talks, I was standing outside in the parking lot in the bright hot sun, and there were some other conference attendees talking to a priest. I walked over so I could listen in. The priest, a relatively young man, was telling the young listeners what he had been doing the past year or so. He described how he had given away virtually all his possessions to the needy. In one instance, a down-on-his-luck guy was without a vehicle. The priest said that God convicted him then and there to hand the keys to his new truck to this man. He obeyed. He also said that he had given away his mattress and bed to someone else. Since then, he had been sleeping on the hard floor.

There is also a beautiful true story, told by William Lane Craig, of a blind, deaf, immobile, deformed 89-year-old woman named Mabel.[23] Despite being trapped in her own body for a quarter century, she was so in love with Jesus and had much joy in her heart. She firmly believed that Jesus was extremely good to her in her life, an amazing mindset given all her infirmities.

---

[23] William Lane Craig, http://www.reasonablefaith.org/defenders-2-podcast/transcript/s4-35.

Pascal's Wager

There's a famous wager about God's existence credited to Blaise Pascal. It argues that it is better for someone unsure about God's existence to believe in Him than not to. For if God does exist, then he has "guessed" correctly and can enjoy the blessings of an afterlife with God. However, if he guesses incorrectly and God does not actually exist, then he has lost nothing. But, on the other hand, if he guesses that God does not exist, and doesn't believe in God, and it turns out that God does indeed exist, then he has lost everything. He has lost the right to go to heaven and in fact may suffer eternity in hell.

At first thought, this argument seems to be making a great point to "hedge your bet". But there are several problems with this argument. One that came to my mind soon after first hearing Pascal's Wager was the question of which God one is supposed to believe in. What if the God of Islam, Allah, is the true God, and someone unsure of whether God exists decides to believe that Jesus Christ is God? According to Islam, that person would be ascribing a partner to God, which is a grave sin. So, if Islam is true, it would be better for that person to remain unsure about God than to believe that Jesus, who Islam considers a great prophet but not God, to be equal to Allah.

There are actually many other problems with Pascal's Wager. See http://infidels.org/library/modern/theism/wager.html for a list of these problems.

Miracles

Then there's the subject of miracles. Has everything occurred according to natural laws, or has God intervened in history at times and circumvented the laws of physics to prove His existence and power?

The Bible is replete with stories of miracles. From the great parting of the Red Sea which allowed God's chosen people to escape the Pharaoh's army, to Moses's staff turning into a snake, to the Resurrection of Jesus Himself, there are numerous amazing suspensions of the laws of nature detailed in Scripture.

But can we believe these miracle stories? Did they actually occur, or were they just fables? And what about the claims of miracles in modern times? Do we have good reason to believe that they are true?

In 2011, New Testament professor Craig S. Keener published a large two-volume set entitled 'Miracles: The Credibility of the New Testament Accounts'. In it he devotes a lot of pages to contemporary claims of supposed medical miracles: bones that are healed, cancers that inexplicably disappear, etc.

As someone who desperately wants to know that a divine miracle has in fact occurred at some time, somewhere, so that belief in God is more than wishful thinking, I am extremely interested in knowing what evidence we have for miracles. I know, however, that even in the 21st century, there is so much we don't know about the internals of the human body and how healing occurs. For this reason, I am skeptical of claims of medical miracles. I am looking instead for evidence of external physical miracles, ones for which there is no natural explanation. About a year ago, I had the opportunity to ask Dr. Keener himself about this. I asked him in an online forum whether he is aware of any contemporary, non-medical miracles. To my dismay, he did not. He has written a tome on miracles and yet he knows of no contemporary evidenced miracle claims that are prominently visible externally. Nothing like a burning bush or a river parting or anything else that doesn't involve the hidden internals of the body.

For those times that I believe that God *is* on his throne, I think that God still performs miracles, but He does them privately to individuals. I will mention one that I believe happened to me.

For a long time, my wife and I did not tithe. That is, we did not give 10% of our income to our church. I know that many Christian pastors and theologians believe that Christians today should tithe, but I didn't know if it was biblical. The reason I felt that way was because of a home pastor in New Jersey that I met about ten years ago who wrote a paper[24] claiming that tithing is not a practice that Christians are instructed to follow. The pastor is Douglas Presley and he writes:

> *Tithing is not grace giving. Tithe means ten percent, or a tenth. The moment we suggest a believer tithe, we are violating the principle of 2 Cor 9:7 … where he is to give "as he has decided in his own heart".*

But my wife kept insisting that we start tithing. And our church had given out free copies of a book advocating for tithing,[25] a book that talked about how the author could not "out-give" God. When he tithed, he miraculously got "reimbursed" for his giving. So, reluctantly, I finally gave in

---

[24] http://www.wordistruth.com/pdf/GivingPolicy.pdf
[25] *The Blessed Life: The Simple Secret of Achieving Guaranteed Financial Results*, Robert Morris, Regal, 2004.

to my wife's wishes. One Sunday a few years ago, I wrote a sizable check for our first tithing check and dropped it in the offering bucket.

The next day, the very next morning - Monday morning - my company had a drawing for a bonus for all those who had submitted their timesheets on time for the five days the previous week. As I scrolled down the email to see who had won, the email kept us in suspense by having a lot of blank lines before it showed the winner. I had the overwhelming, eerie feeling that I knew I was the winner. Sure enough – there was my name at the bottom of the email! And what monetary bonus had I won? **Exactly** the same amount I had tithed the day before! Now it wasn't an odd amount, like so many dollars and 37 cents, but it was still the exact amount I had tithed. This amazed me. And it showed that I could not out-give God!

Now, was this just an amazing coincidence? Perhaps – but I didn't consider it so. I wasn't going to doubt that this was a sign from God. So, even though I couldn't argue that tithing was right for all Christians, it seemed to be what God wanted for my family, so we continued to tithe after that.

5

Is Jesus Christ God?

"Jesus never said the exact three words, 'I am God.'"
-- Matt Slick, Christian Apologetics & Research Ministry

"… we wait for the blessed hope—the appearing of the glory of our great God and Savior, Jesus Christ"
-- Titus 2:13, NIV

Cliffe is asked various questions about why he is a Christian and why the rest of us should be. For this, Cliffe offers several reasons why he is a follower of Christ.

Christ's Lifestyle

Christ lived a life beyond reproach. According to the Bible, He was the only human being up until then, or since, who lived into adulthood without sinning. That's just one person who succeeded out of the some 100,000,000,000 people that science believes has ever been born. Jesus lived to age 33, so for 15-20 or more years that He knew right from wrong, he never once told a lie, or had a lustful thought that He didn't immediately dispel with, or cheated anybody on anything.

Christ treated people with love and compassion. I think of the story where the Jewish leaders took a woman caught in adultery to Jesus to have her stoned[26]. He showed compassion on her by instructing the men around her with this:

"He that is without sin among you, let him be the first to cast a stone at her."[27]

Christ's Ethical Teachings

Cliffe says that Jesus's ethical teachings have the "ring of truth", that they are profound. He quotes Robert Coles, psychology professor at Harvard, who has said "All the writings on ethics over the past 2,000 years are simply footnotes to the Sermon on the Mount".

Christ's Death

When Christ was put to death by the Romans by means of crucifixion, an extremely cruel and torturous process, Christ forgave, rather than cursed, His persecutors:

"Father, forgive them; for they know not what they do."[28]

This is an amazing display of grace and forgiveness toward people who were brutally beating and killing Jesus.

Christ's Resurrection

Cliffe points out that the Resurrection shows tremendous credibility for the divinity of Jesus and the reliability of the

---

[26] John 8:2-11.
[27] John 8:7, Jubilee Bible 2000.
[28] Luke 23:34, KJV.

Bible. To him, the actual physical resurrection of Jesus from the dead is a powerful reason that he's a Christian. It's clearly an impressive event, and it's necessarily a supernatural one, because we know of no one who was once dead, then came back to life, especially without any interaction from another human being.

When Jesus threw the moneychangers and merchants out of His temple in Jerusalem, the Jews there asked Him what sign He could show them to prove His authority to do that. Jesus responded: "Destroy this temple, and I will raise it again in three days. They replied, 'It has taken forty-six years to build this temple, and you are going to raise it in three days?' But the temple he had spoken of was his body."[29] And, sure enough, according to the Bible at least, He was raised on the third day after He was crucified.

Christ's resurrection is a crucial point to whether Christianity is true or not. As the apostle Paul writes, "if Christ has not been raised, our preaching is useless and so is your faith."[30] He also writes "if Christ has not been raised, your faith is futile; you are still in your sins"[31]. Cliffe loves to tell students "If you rise from the dead, I promise to listen very carefully to everything you have to say."

What evidence do we have supporting the Resurrection? Three of the strongest pieces of evidence are the empty tomb, the appearances of Christ after his death, and the thorough transformation of the apostles.

---

[29] John 2:18-21, NIV.
[30] 1 Corinthians 20:15, NIV.
[31] 1 Corinthians 20:17, NIV.

The Historical Reliability of the Bible

Cliffe's belief in the truth of Christianity is also buttressed by the historical reliability of the Bible. He mentions several subpoints here: the internal consistency of the books of the Bible, the narrative literary style used in several books, the archeological evidence that has been uncovered in the two millennia since the time of Jesus, and the Biblical manuscript evidence.

The Bible may very well be internally consistent. In two thousand years, no one has successfully been able to show that there is a contradiction in the Scriptures that cannot be reconciled in some way.

As for literary style, several books of the Bible are written as a narrative, namely Genesis, Exodus, Numbers, Joshua, Judges, 1 & 2 Samuel, 1 & 2 Kings, 1 & 2 Chronicles, Ruth, Ezra, Nehemiah, Daniel, Jonah, Haggai, some of the Prophetic writings, the Gospels (Matthew, Mark, Luke, and John), and the Acts of the Apostles.[32]

Regarding archeological evidence, a very large amount has been discovered since the Bible was written which corroborates it. For instance, there are dozens of verses in the Bible that refer to the Hittites. But up until the late 1800s the Hittites were thought to be just a Biblical invention. Then several archeological discoveries revealed not only the existence of the Hittite kingdom for roughly 400 years beginning in 1600BC, but also its great scale and power.

One argument for Christianity which I was taught and which always bolstered my faith was the claim that nearly all of the

---

[32] 'Understanding the Literary Type or Genre of the Books of the Bible, http://prepareinternational.org/wp-content/uploads/2009/12/e-understandingthegenreofthebook.pdf.

twelve apostles were martyred for their faith. Now there are people who will die for something they believe to be true, but these men supposedly died for what they believed they had *seen*. This is a very much stronger testament to the validity of a claim, for it does not rely on other people's testimony.

Unfortunately however, the evidence that the apostles were martyred for their faith is not nearly as strong as I had been told. For many of the original twelve apostles (Peter, Andrew, James, John, Philip, Bartholomew, Thomas, Matthew, James the son of Alphaeus, Thaddaeus, Simon, and Judas), we only have late and legendary evidence[33]. We can be somewhat confident that Peter was martyred[34], as was Stephen[35]. But the evidence for the martyrdom of most of the ten other apostles is not as strong.

---

[33] Josh McDowell, 'Did the Apostles Really Die as Martyrs for their Faith?', Biola Magazine, Fall 2013.
[34] John 21:18-19; Tertullian in the 2nd century; Origen in the 3rd century.
[35] Acts 7:54-60.

6

Is Hell Just?

"The New Testament teaches that the vast majority of the men, women, and children who have lived on earth are in Hell suffering endless torment and will remain in this condition forever. To believe this is to make the Christian God a monster beyond imagining."
--Charles Templeton, 'Farewell to God: My Reasons for Rejecting the Christian Faith'

"The God that holds you over the pit of hell, much as one holds a spider, or some loathsome insect over the fire, abhors you, and is dreadfully provoked: his wrath towards you burns like fire; he looks upon you as worthy of nothing else, but to be cast into the fire; he is of purer eyes than to bear to have you in his sight; you are ten thousand times more abominable in his eyes, than the most hateful venomous serpent is in ours. You have offended him infinitely more than ever a stubborn rebel did his prince; and yet it is nothing but his hand that holds you from falling into the fire every moment."
--Jonathan Edwards, 18th-century "fire and brimstone" preacher

One theme I hear brought up a lot is the concept of God's justice. Students will object that it is patently unfair that a terrible individual can live a life of evil and sadism, only to accept Jesus on his deathbed and thereby be saved, opening up heaven to this person for all eternity, allowing him to not suffer any of the torments he inflicted people with while on this earth.

This doctrine does seem horribly, innately unfair. Consider Ted Bundy, the infamous serial killer who kidnapped, raped, murdered, and post-mortemly violated dozens of girls and young women. According to James Dobson of Focus on the

Family, Ted Bundy accepted Christ in prison soon before he was put to death, thanks to James Dobson himself! The thought that a monster such as Bundy can torture and kill many people and then be "rewarded" by being welcomed into heaven is a truly repugnant thought. Combine this with the realization that perhaps several of Bundy's own victims were murdered by him before they received salvation makes the whole situation nauseating to say the least.

Cliffe responds to this question by bringing up two points. First, he points out that, in God's eyes, none of us are good. "there is no one who does good, not even one"[36], and "all our righteous acts are like filthy rags"[37]. Using these verses as the moral yardstick, the contention is that none of us deserve heaven. So the question becomes then, not why some very bad people can end up in heaven, but why any one of us, no matter how saintly, deserve heaven as our final destination.

Secondly, Cliffe informs the questioner that Jesus's death on the cross is sufficient to atone for our sins, no matter how evil we have been. This covers then the Ted Bundy's, the Jeffrey Dahmer's, even the Adolf Hitler's.

On the other side of the equation, students will point to Mahatma Gandhi as someone who, although he led a very good and moral life, since he didn't become a Christian, is currently and forever in hell, or will be in hell forever. Cliffe replies by reiterating that there is no one good in God's eyes, and also that we can't easily judge the hearts of others. But the Bible also talks about a person being judged more leniently if he doesn't know the Truth. Luke 12:47-48a says "The servant who knows the master's will and does not get ready or does not do what the master wants will be beaten

---

[36] Psalms 14:3, NIV.
[37] Isaiah 64:6, NIV.

with many blows. But the one who does not know and does things deserving punishment will be beaten with few blows."

Cliffe also tells a story highlighting God's authority and the gravity of sinning against God. In Give Me An Answer's YouTube episode #1114, Cliffe gives the example of a child who kicks sand in another kid's face in a sandbox. The teacher comes over and scolds the child for this, after which the child just hauls back and slaps the teacher. The kid is then brought to the principal's office and told he did a bad thing. The little imp now just slaps the principal. Now he's in real trouble. A policeman shows up and the kid just hauls back and punches the officer. Now the kid's going to jail. When he gets out, he goes and sees the President of the United States. He hauls back to smack the President when the Secret Service shoots him dead. Now why is the punishment worse for trying to smack the President than kicking sand in another kid's face? Cliffe says it is because of the authority of the office of the President. Likewise when we sin against God. Each violation against God, no matter how minor it seems to us, is a major offense, because we are sinning against the all-powerful, all-holy Creator of the Universe. I feel though that this analogy does not work very well though because, in God's eyes, each action of the child in this story is a sin against God, not just a sin against the particular person.

I've always found the concept of an eternal, conscious hell to be monstrous. How could an earthly lifetime spent rejecting Christ's salvific message possibly deserve an infinite hereafter in excruciating pain or suffering? Charles Templeton, the late great evangelist who toured internationally with Billy Graham but later became an agnostic, said to Lee Strobel during his interview for Strobel's excellent book 'The Case For Faith': "I couldn't hold someone's hand to a fire for a moment. Not an instant! How could a loving God, just because you don't obey him and do what he wants, torture you forever - not allowing you to die, but to continue in that pain for eternity. There's no criminal on earth who would do this!"[38]

Perhaps hell, being often defined as a "separation from God", is actually nonexistence. Perhaps instead of suffering eternal torment, the unsaved are annihilated by God – they just cease to exist. There are many Bible verses which can be used to argue this claim. One of them is Malachi 4:1, which says that "the arrogant people who do evil things will be burned up like stove wood, burned to a crisp, nothing left but scorched earth and ash" (The Message Bible). This certainly reads like annihilation, doesn't it? There are many other verses in the New Testament that talk about "destruction" of the soul in hell, and of the souls of unbelievers being "consumed", implying annihilation.[39]

Some claim that we cannot be annihilated because we are made in God's image, and God is an eternal spirit. But certainly God can spare the torment of the untold billions of people who have ever lived whose life transpired without being redeemed. If God just extinguished the flames of these people's souls, He would not be violating His character of justice – they still would not be granted access to His presence in heaven.

Along this line of thinking, one student at the University of Arizona asked Cliffe if we can choose to "just die" instead of going to either heaven or hell. Cliffe says no, that God has decided not to give people that choice, just like He has decided not to give people the choice of whether they wanted to be born or not.

---

[38] http://www.valleyviewseek.org/loving-send-people-hell, accessed February 25, 2015.
[39] Mt 7:19, 13:40; Jn 15:6, Heb 6:8, 10:7.

For another alternative, the Roman Catholic concept of purgatory sounds palatable regarding this issue. When a person dies in a "state of grace", he or she goes to a place of punishment for a certain amount of time based on the amount and severity of sins he or she committed during his or her life. After that period, the person is forever admitted to heaven. Of course, just because this idea sounds palatable, it doesn't mean that it is true. Catholics point to various Bible verses for justification of their belief in purgatory, including Mt 5:24-25 and the deuterocanonical II Maccabees 12:39-46.

There are those that believe that heaven and hell are man-made concepts. They believe that the masses of people in history that lived a very hard and often tragic short life needed to believe in a place that would make up for the suffering they lived through in this life. They needed hope for the future, even if that future meant a future beyond their current life. Without this hope, many more surely would have committed suicide throughout history.

Likewise for hell. When a terrible king or dictator is responsible for your lousy life, or for the deaths of some of your family members, and you know that they aren't likely to pay for their actions in this life, the concept that they would get their due punishment in a future life of torment would be highly attractive, would it not? Perhaps the idea of hell developed over time for this reason.

One question that I've had about hell for many years, and which I've posed to a few people from time to time, is this: Would you have, say, 10 kids knowing beforehand that even just one would go to hell (assuming hell is a place of eternal conscious agony)? I would have a hard time sleeping at night knowing that someone I brought into this world would suffer in an eternal conscious hell.

Now, according to the Bible, the vast majority of people end up going to hell:

"Enter through the narrow gate. For wide is the gate and broad is the road that leads to destruction, and many enter through it. But small is the gate and narrow the road that leads to life, and only a few find it."[40]

But let's say you have a strong Christian influence on your children, so that only one of your ten kids don't become saved during their lifetime. Even with a 90% success rate, would you still conceive those kids knowing that one would spend an eternity in hell? Or would you instead stay childless so that you aren't (at least partially) responsible for sending a soul to hell? Personally, I wouldn't have those kids. I would sacrifice my joy of having children, of having progeny, for the sake of that one child. It seems to me to be terribly cruel to do otherwise. Even though that child would have the chance to accept Jesus's payment for his sins during his lifetime, the fact remains that that child would not end up in hell if I did not have him. I would knowingly want no part in that outcome.

Then there is the question of the fate of those who have not heard of Jesus. This is a common question posed to Cliffe, for which he responds that ultimately he does not know. But then he's quick to point out that the Bible mentions a number of people who have not heard of Jesus yet are in heaven. From Hebrews chapter 11, there's Abraham, Isaac, Jacob, Moses, David, and Rahab the Gentile prostitute. There are certainly many Christians and Christian theologians who feel strongly that anyone who hasn't heard of Jesus cannot be saved, since John 14:6 says "I am the way and the truth and the life. No one comes to the Father except through me"

---

[40] Matthew 7:13-14, NIV.

and Acts 4:12 says "there is no other name under heaven given to mankind by which we must be saved".

One student asked Cliffe "What if we're just dead after we die?" Cliffe responded by saying that, if we're just dead after we die, then Hitler and Mother Teresa are in the same place (the grave), that what you do in this life is ultimately meaningless; that it doesn't matter how one lives their life. I see the point here, although I would add that, even if God exists and there's a heaven and hell, it doesn't matter for many how they live their life. Take Ted Bundy again, who lived his life in the most evil of ways, and yet supposedly received a pardon at the end and is now in heaven.

On a related note, Cliffe wonders sometimes why God withholds his judgment against America. I assume Cliffe feels that the moral fabric of the United States has deteriorated significantly in the last several decades, and that God may soon remove His protective hand over America. I understand this point, and I also agree that in many ways America seems to be in moral decline. I do however believe we romanticize earlier times in America perhaps too much. It wasn't all Norman Rockwell. We think of the manners we had, we think of the chivalry, we think of the general God-fearing we had. But what about the sexism? What about the racism? Both were arguably worse in the past. And what about the wanton violence in the Prohibition era and the Wild West?

The truth is, if God judges or protects nations based on their goodness, wouldn't America still today be near the end of the line among the 200+ nations to be judged? What about all the nations where believing in the name of Jesus as Lord is persecuted or even outlawed?

7

Why Is There So Much Pain And Suffering?

"God whispers to us in our pleasures, speaks in our conscience, but shouts in our pain; it is His megaphone to rouse a deaf world."
-- C.S. Lewis, The Problem of Pain (New York: HarperCollins, 1940/1996), 91.

"As long as there is one person suffering an injustice; as long as one person is forced to bear an unnecessary sorrow; as long as one person is subject to an undeserved pain, the worship of a God is a demoralizing humiliation."
-- Joseph Lewis, An Atheist Manifesto (CreateSpace, 2012).

Wars. Torture. Violence. Rape. Disease. Natural tragedy. The world is awash in pain and suffering, and almost always has been. This is traditionally the strongest argument against the existence of an omniscient (all-knowing), omnipotent (all-powerful), and omnibenevolent (all-good) God. Personally, it has been the most difficult obstacle to me to maintain a strong faith in the existence of a loving God. Whenever I ruminate on the appalling extent and pervasiveness of pain and suffering *currently* occurring in the world, not to mention what has transpired throughout the history of man on earth, I often have a feeling that it is ludicrous to even believe in God. Sometimes I feel that it is monstrous of me and other Christians just to believe in a God who would allow the amount and severity of pain and suffering which has occurred throughout history, and who has at times even *commanded* violent acts. I can empathize with Friedrich Nietzsche's words: "The only excuse for God is that he doesn't exist."

This argument against the existence of the Judeo-Christian God as described in the Bible is very old. In recorded history, it can be traced back at least to the ancient Greek philosopher Epicurus (341 BC - 270 BC), who phrased the problem as such:

Is God willing to prevent evil, but not able?
    Then he is not omnipotent.
Is he able, but not willing?
    Then he is malevolent.
Is he both able and willing?
    Then whence cometh evil?
Is he neither able nor willing?
    Then why call him God?

Cliffe has admitted that this is a strong argument[41], perhaps the strongest argument against the existence of the Christian God.

Cliffe has been hammered with questions on this topic many times over the years in his college ministry. He offers various responses, depending on the question and sometimes on the emotional demeanor of the student doing the asking. Sometimes Cliffe responds with his signature "I … do … not … know" reply, which is an understandable response to questions which have, in all honesty, not found adequate answers across the millennia. Other times, Cliffe attempts to defend his belief in a good God with the reality of so much pain and suffering in the world. The main point he raises is the concept of free will, that ultimately we are responsible for

---

[41] Debate with Michael Newdow, December 8, 2002. See Appendix C for details and a summary of the debate.

the awful state of affairs we find ourselves in. I devote a later chapter to free will.

Why does all this evil exist? Christians say that it is because of The Fall, that pivotal moment when the first two humans, Adam and Eve, chose to disobey and eat of the Tree of the Knowledge of Good and Evil[42]. That one act created a chasm between God and man, a rift that is responsible for all the pain and suffering that has followed.

This is a difficult piece of doctrine. It flies in the face of what we inherently understand in Western cultures as justice, for how can the transgression of one who lived so many generations prior mean that his distant progeny be held responsible? In Western judicial systems, people aren't held morally culpable for the crimes committed by their parents or ancestors. They may suffer the consequences of them, like being poor or ostracized from the family, but they are not morally responsible for the "sins of the father". This is the Christian doctrine of "original sin". We are all born stained with sin. We are all guilty "right out of the gate".

So Christianity teaches that we are responsible for the sin of mankind's first couple. This is the doctrine of Original Sin. There are several reasons for this transference of blame. One is the belief that Adam and Eve's souls were tainted by their disobedience to God, and this stain of sin is handed down spiritually to their offspring - the entire human race. Another reason given is that, whether or not we are stained by sin at birth, we all at some point go astray and therefore become guilty. This is a difficult doctrine, and there are Bible verses that can be used to argue for or against Original Sin.

How do we become "unstained" by sin? We do this by repenting ("turning from") our sin and believing in the

---

[42] Genesis 3.

salvific work of Jesus Christ on the cross. Jesus, a sinless human after some 33 years of life, and God's own son, sacrificed His own life on a brutal Roman cross (or stake) roughly 2,000 years ago on the mount of Calvary. This sacrifice from the Lamb of God was sufficient payment to the all-just Father for the sins of all mankind for all times.

Another topic related to pain and suffering is the atrocities in the Old Testament, of which there are many. One of them was the slaughter of the Amalekites. In 1 Samuel 15, God tells King Saul through the prophet Samuel to "attack the Amalekites and totally destroy all that belongs to them. Do not spare them; put to death men and women, children and infants, cattle and sheep, camels and donkeys." This is God commanding the slaughter of children and infants! How could a good God do this?

This obviously is an extremely difficult passage to swallow. But most difficult stories in the Bible are made less unpalatable when they are put into context. As for the Amalekites, they had attacked the Israelites earlier, several times in fact[43], so God wished to punish them, and did not want remnants of their group left to further threaten His chosen people. Cliffe also has responded that we are all interconnected as human beings, so God judges people groups even though there are innocents that get hurt in the process.

Then there is the story of Uzzah, who was struck dead in an instant by God merely for touching the Ark of the Covenant to prevent it from falling when the oxen pulling it stumbled[44]. So here was a man who was trying to **prevent** the holy Ark from crashing to the ground, and yet God killed him anyway.

---

[43] Numbers 14:45, Judges 3:13, Judges 6-7.
[44] 2 Samuel 6:6-7, 1 Chronicles 13:9-10.

This is also a tough story to understand. Why would God strike down a man who was reaching out to protect His holy Ark? The reason is that God gave specific instructions on how the Ark was to be handled, and by whom. These instructions were not followed, which is a big insult to God and His holy name. It showed a lack of reverence for God and His holy artifacts. God gave Moses and Aaron specific instructions about the handling and movement of the Ark, warning that whoever touched the Ark would die.

As I mentioned in the Introduction, it's not just that my name is Christian - I am a Christian. And yet, this perpetual Problem of Evil often makes me doubt the existence of God. If I watch the news for five minutes, or browse the Internet for a little while, I often get that sinking feeling in the pit of my stomach that "this is just too much", that it is preposterous that a loving God exists. Murder, famine, genocide, terrorism, etc. It is insane how much pain and suffering exists, and has existed since the beginning of life on earth. Everyone is familiar with famous atrocities such as the Nazi Holocaust or the Rwandan massacre, but there are plenty of lesser-known realities that may, unbelievably, be even more immediately gut-wrenching. I hesitate to mention these, but I want to include them to show just how difficult belief in a good God can often be. Those of a sensitive nature may want to skip the next few paragraphs.

In World War II, in the Auschwitz concentration camp, amidst the despair and horrible events that was the hell of Auschwitz, three Jewish rabbis who were prisoners decided to conduct a formal trial against ... God! They tried Him in absentia for abandoning His chosen people. The question at hand was whether God had broken His holy covenant with the Jewish people by allowing the Nazis to commit genocide. Elie Wiesel, famous Auschwitz survivor, recalled this trial when he was there as a teenager. According to American theologian Robert McAfee Brown:

> *The trial lasted several nights. Witnesses were heard, evidence was gathered, conclusions were drawn, all of which issued finally in a unanimous verdict: the Lord God Almighty, Creator of Heaven and Earth, was found guilty of crimes against creation and humankind.*[45]

Even the animal kingdom is fraught with horrific examples of almost unfathomable cruelty. Let me mention just a couple. The first is gruesome, the second even more horrific.

The lancet fluke is a small parasite which invades and actually controls the mind of ants. "The adult lancet fluke inhabits the body of a cow, releasing its eggs into the host's feces. Snails, who happen to enjoy a nice hot cow pie, end up eating the eggs and getting infested with worm larvae. The snails react to the larvae by spitting them back out in big balls of slime, and these wormy slimeballs smell incredibly delicious to passing ants. Once eaten by an ant, the worm waits until nightfall when it's nice and cool and forces the ant to climb a blade of grass, bite down on the tip, and raise its butt into the air. This is the perfect position to get swallowed by another cow, and if the ant doesn't get swallowed? The worm releases control in the morning, allows the ant to live a normal day of anthood, and repeats the whole process night after night."[46] Incredibly gruesome, isn't it?

And then there's a very disturbing ongoing situation in East Asia, especially in China. Thousands of black bears are kept in tiny cages, called "crush cages", and milked for their bile, to be used in traditional Chinese medicine.[47] The cages are so small that the bears cannot stand up or move around. This horrible practice often involves making a permanent hole in the bear's abdomen and gall bladder to allow the bile to just

---

[45] From http://en.wikipedia.org/wiki/Elie_Wiesel
[46] http://www.toptenz.net/top-10-zombie-parasites.php
[47] http://en.wikipedia.org/wiki/Bile_bear

freely drip out for collection. Sometimes the hole is kept open with a catheter, causing constant terrible pain to the bear. A report from August 2011[48] said that a mother bear, in order to spare her cub from a life of such torture, intentionally strangled her cub, then killed herself by running head first into a wall. This story bothers me greatly, and has made me wonder how we could have a loving God who allows this to occur.

Charles Templeton admitted that the existence of so much extreme pain and suffering is what made him doubt and eventually discard his Christian faith. He saw a photograph in LIFE magazine of an anguished mother in Africa who was wailing while holding her dead child, who had died from a lack of rainwater for drinking. Templeton believed then that it was impossible to believe in a benevolent God who would allow children like this to die when all that was needed was some rain to fall.[49]

There is some tragic irony regarding this subject worth mentioning. One of Cliffe's favorite campuses to visit is the great University of Texas in Austin. That is where I saw him last, in the fall of 2010. Cliffe speaks there at the base of the steps on the West side of the UT Tower, with the student listeners sitting on the steps as if they were bleachers. This is exactly the location of one of the worst mass shootings in US history. On the afternoon of August 1, 1966, ex-UT student Charles Whitman entered the UT Tower with several rifles and shotguns, took the elevator to its highest level on the 27th floor, climbed the single flight of stairs to the observation deck, and then proceeded to shoot roughly 40 people on the ground below, killing 11[50].

---

[48] http://www.dailymail.co.uk/news/article-2025388/China-Tortured-mother-bear-kills-cub-herself.html
[49] http://www.valleyviewseek.org/good-world
[50] https://en.wikipedia.org/wiki/Charles_Whitman

One poignant book of the Bible which deals with suffering is the book of Job. Job was a man of great faith who suffered inconceivably as the result of a wager between God and Satan. The Devil felt that Job only feared and worshipped God because he was living a charmed life, without trials and tribulations. God denied this and, to prove it to Satan and to people throughout history who would hear or read this story, God allowed Satan to kill all ten of his children, his thousands of livestock, and then to afflict Job with horrible ailments. Job was covered with boils over his entire body – boils so painful that he scraped his skin with broken pottery to try to lessen the pain. He lost everything – his children, his possessions, and his good health. And yet the Bible says he still did not curse God.

Yet Job certainly wondered why he had to suffer so. He cried out to God "Why have you made me your target? Have I become a burden to you?"[51] And "Does it please you to oppress me?"[52] He wonders why he was even born: "Why then did you bring me out of the womb? I wish I had died before any eye saw me."[53]

I've long been bothered by this trial that God allowed Job to go through. Since God knew Job would be faithful to Him, He could have just imbued or imparted to Satan the knowledge of how Job would act had he been afflicted with the trials Satan were to impose. God could have certainly won the challenge without the need for Job to go through such pain and misery. Is this story true? Was a man named Job really a pawn in a cosmic battle between God and the Evil One?

---

[51] Job 7:20b, NIV.
[52] Job 10:3a, NIV.
[53] Job 10:18, NIV.

Regarding death, Cliffe brings up that it is not the worst thing that can happen to a person. Not being saved would be far worse. If hell exists and is eternal and conscious, then that is a vast understatement. Dying without being redeemed by Jesus's death on the cross would literally be a fate worse than death. For even if one's life in this world is horrible, it is temporary, lasting less than 100 years for the vast majority of us, often much less. And yet it wouldn't even compare to the agony of an infinite amount of time in hell.

Cliffe also points out that death can be a compassionate end for someone who is suffering terribly. That of course assumes that that person is a believer bound for heaven. That is certainly true. In many cases, the body of a person who is physically suffering tremendously eventually gives out, putting an end to that person's suffering on Earth.

The Devil himself also shares responsibility for the presence of pain and suffering in this world. He had a hand in turning Judas, one of Jesus's original twelve apostles, against the Lord and handing Him over to be tried and executed. Satan is described as one who "prowls around like a roaring lion, seeking someone to devour"[54].

Further Reading

There are numerous books on the Problem of Evil and Suffering. Here are a few notable ones:

From a Christian perspective:

Where Is God When It Hurts, Philip Yancey, Zondervan, 2002.

---

[54] 1 Peter 5:8, ESV.

The Gift Of Pain, Paul Brand and Philip Yancey, Zondervan, 1997.

The Problem of Pain, C.S. Lewis, HarperOne, 2009.

A Grief Observed, C.S. Lewis, HarperOne, 2009.

If God, Why Evil?: A New Way to Think About the Question, Norman L. Geisler, Bethany House Publishers, 2011.

From an atheist perspective:

God's Problem: How the Bible Fails to Answer Our Most Important Question--Why We Suffer, Bart Ehrman, HarperOne, 2009.

8

What's Wrong With Sex?

"Sex is a part of nature. I go along with nature."
-- Marilyn Monroe

"Flee from sexual immorality. All other sins a person commits are outside the body, but whoever sins sexually, sins against their own body."
--1 Corinthians 6:18

Being an open-air evangelist speaking on college campuses, Cliffe understandably is asked a fair number of questions regarding sex. Some students ask what is wrong with "hooking up" or having sex with their girlfriend or boyfriend. Others ask what is wrong with homosexuality or bisexuality. And some just ask what is wrong with sexual relations before, or outside of, marriage.

In response, Cliffe informs the college student posing the question that they are "more than just a body", that he or she is a human being, complete with a soul and a personality. And while sex is a very enjoyable gift from God, it is to be enjoyed only in the confines of a marriage between a man and a woman.

One crass comment I heard Cliffe make once was directed to the young men. He said that a woman was not just a vat for a guy's sperm – obviously a very pointed admonition to guys who are selfishly solely looking for a release for their sexual tensions.

It is easy to empathize for young Americans of today and the last several decades though, since the average age for which a man gets married for the first time is 29, and for a woman it is 27[55]. Since boys and girls enter puberty now at increasingly younger ages - the average age is now between 10 and 14 for girls and between 12 and 16 for boys - that means that the average American has to wait up to nearly 20 years from his/her first desire to have sex until he/she can have it according to God's will, which is only in a marital relationship. Contrast that with men and women during Jesus's time, in first-century Palestine. Then, boys and girls usually got married soon after reaching puberty and having their first sexual desires.

So it is asking a lot of young people today to wait until marriage to engage in sex. If waiting so many years until marriage was difficult enough, mass media in American society adds to the difficulty by marketing sex in movies, commercials, music videos, billboards, etc. This has a strong effect. For men, who are especially visually oriented, this elicits sexual desire and lust. Women often respond to this flood of sexually-tinged marketing by purchasing provocative clothing so that they may feel sexier and more easily entice the opposite sex. This all makes obeying the edict from God to save sex for marriage extremely difficult.

There are a significant number of questions asked about homosexuality. Cliffe has been asked why it is wrong for a homosexual couple to be in a monogamous relationship. He has responded with his famous "I … do … not … know" retort, but saying that it is God's law, and ultimately that is what matters.

---

[55]source: U.S. Census Bureau, 2011 American Community Service

I remember about 20 years ago when walking through the student organization floor in the Student Union at the University of Illinois I noticed a big poster on the door of an organization for homosexuals that said across the top something like "What Jesus Said About Homosexuality". The rest of the poster was completely blank. Now Jesus did speak some about other sexual sin[56], but the poster was pointing out that Jesus never directly spoke out against homosexuality specifically.

One verse in the Bible that sounds particularly extreme, and which is apropos to most male college students, is Matthew 5:28: "But I tell you that anyone who looks at a woman lustfully has already committed adultery with her in his heart."[57] It is part of a passage where Jesus is stressing that a person's heart intentions are in a certain sense as serious as the actual carrying out of the actual sin. This verse is one of the most common ones used by campus preachers to provoke and engage their student audiences. I noticed that Cliffe's bible is open to this verse in the opening musical montage near the beginning of each of his newer YouTube videos. I don't believe this is just a matter of coincidence.

---

[56] See Mt 5:27-29 and Jn 8:1-11.
[57] NIV.

9

Do We Have Free Will?

"A moment or two of serious self-scrutiny, and you might observe that you no more decide the next thought you think than the next thought I write."
— Sam Harris, Free Will

"Why, then, did God give them [people] free will? Because free will, though it makes evil possible, is also the only thing that makes possible any love or goodness or joy worth having. A world of automata - of creatures that worked like machines - would hardly be worth creating."
— C.S. Lewis, The Case for Christianity

Another point which Cliffe uses as evidence that there is a God is the idea of determinism versus free will. Cliffe argues that, if there is no God, then we are basically just robots, with all of our actions predetermined by initial conditions and subsequent events. Without God, Cliffe claims that we have no free will - that determinism rules the day. Every action we perform, every thought we think, is predetermined. But this is disturbing, because we naturally like to feel that we decide things for ourselves.

Cliffe points out that, without God, we are "just matter and energy evolved to a higher order" - we are just a series of biochemical reactions. His intention here is clearly to make students feel that determinism must not be true since each of us innately feels that we are making our own decisions, that we are not compelled to decide to do choice A over choice B due to pre-programming in our brain. However, just because the thought that we are determined solely by our physical makeup and the collective set of the past events in our life is unpalatable does not mean that it cannot be so.

Similarly for emotions such as love. If determinism is correct, then love is just a biochemical reaction. When a girl tells her boyfriend that she loves him, she is just letting him know that her biochemical reactions are firing in such a way that she *feels* that she is in love with him. She isn't *choosing* to love her boyfriend – she is merely determined, or programmed, to "love" him.

Cliffe regularly tells a story of a young woman who is dating a young man. One day the father of the woman shocks her by informing her that he has been paying her boyfriend $1,000 a week to date her. How would this revelation make the young woman feel? She would feel angry and sad, of course - angry at her father for paying her boyfriend to date her and sad that her boyfriend wasn't dating her because he was interested in her as a person.

The question of whether determinism is reality is a difficult problem. Perhaps determinism does in fact rule the day. Perhaps our thoughts are just the culmination of all the innumerable events that came before them. How do we know that this is not the case? We really don't, do we?

A 2008 study from the Max Planck Institute for Human Cognitive and Brain Sciences in Leipzig, Germany suggests that free will might just be an illusion.[58] Their study showed that the brain "makes up its mind" up to ten seconds before the person realizes it. That is, parts of the brain are making a decision well before the person believes he or she is making that decision. The researchers knew what the person decided

---

[58] http://www.mpg.de/567905/pressRelease20080414

before they themselves did. This seems to imply that we do not in fact have free will.

A student has asked Cliffe "How can we have free will if God knows how we will choose?" If our decisions are known to God beforehand, then do we really have the free will to decide A over B? This objection seems to be a valid point at first, until one realizes that God is an eternal being. Being eternal means He is "outside of time". He can look at the whole timeline of history and see all points "simultaneously". Even though He doesn't dictate what decisions you and I make, He nonetheless can see what we will choose at all points of our life.

Further Reading

From a Christian perspective:

'Mind, Brain, and Free Will' by Richard Swinburne, 2013, 288pp.

'Four Views on Free Will', Fischer, Kane, Pereboom, & Vargas, Wiley-Blackwell, 2007, 240pp.

From an atheist perspective:

'Free Will' by Sam Harris, Free Press, 2012, 96pp.

10

Creation Or Evolution?

"Evolution is a bankrupt speculative philosophy, not a scientific fact. Only a spiritually bankrupt society could ever believe it. ... Only atheists could accept this Satanic theory."
- Rev. Jimmy Swaggart

"To put it bluntly but fairly, anyone today who doubts that the variety of life on this planet was produced by a process of evolution is simply ignorant—inexcusably ignorant, in a world where three out of four people have learned to read and write."
— Daniel C. Dennett, Darwin's Dangerous Idea: Evolution and the Meanings of Life

"Well I'll be a monkey's uncle!"
– common saying following the famous 1925 Scopes "monkey trial"

Most students at non-Christian colleges believe in Darwinian evolution. That is what they are taught if they attended a public high school, and that is what they are taught in secular colleges. As a Catholic who attended secular elementary education, I believed in God, and I also believed in evolution. I believed in what is known as theistic evolution, the concept that God used evolution to create the diversity of life. God kicked off the process, then evolution including natural selection took its course, leading up to the development of us, homo sapiens.

Cliffe counters by saying that, if evolution is true and there also is no God, then life must have come from non-life. He says this phenomenon has never been shown to occur. This is true. Despite centuries of attempts at creating life from nonlife, none have been successful. There have been impressive results though. In 1953, Stanley Miller and Harold Urey at the University of Chicago succeeded in showing that organic compounds can be formed from inorganic precursors in conditions that may have resembled those of the early Earth. Some 25 different amino acids were formed in these experiments, according to sealed vials that have only recently been opened and investigated. For comparison, all life uses just 20 different amino acids.

There are also the fundamental physical constants of the universe which, if they varied only extremely slightly, an evolutionary universe wouldn't permit the formation of life. There are dozens of these constants, each of which, if they only differed ever so slightly from their actual value, might not allow for the universe as we know it. For example, galaxies and stars might not exist, or life might not exist.

Let's look at one of these constants, the ratio of the number of protons to electrons in the universe. This ratio is extremely close to 1. It has been theorized that if the true ratio was off by just 1 part in 10^{37} (that's 1 part in 10,000,000,000,000,000,000,000,000,000,000,000,000), then electromagnetic forces would overwhelm gravitational forces, preventing the formation of galaxies, stars, and planets.

Due to the extreme lack of leeway in the values of these constants, William Lane Craig has said that "scientifically speaking, it's far more probable for a life-prohibiting universe to exist than a life-sustaining one. Life is balanced on a razor's edge."[59] This seems to be a strong argument for the existence of an intelligent Creator of the universe. If the universe came

---

[59] http://www.reasonablefaith.org/transcript-fine-tuning-argument, accessed February 25, 2015.

about from purely natural causes, then values of many physical constants should be able to range over wide values, in which case it is mathematically absurd that the precise values we see today could have arisen.

Perhaps the only way for the God-denier to account for these precise cosmic values is to postulate the existence of a multiverse. With this idea, there are a very large number of parallel universes (even an infinite number – an 'infiniverse') where each universe represents a different combination of values of the fundamental physical constants. Then, in one of these universes (the one we reside in), the combination of values is just right to allow for the origination and flourishing of life. So, even though *our* universe seems to be fine-tuned for life, it is merely part of a larger system that is not fine-tuned.

Regarding God, Cliffe says that if there is no God, then we as humans are just "primordial slime evolved to a higher order", or "pond scum evolved to a higher order". Yes, but why the hate for pond scum? Pond scum are people too! All kidding aside, why is it insulting to believe that man evolved from ancestors of the chimpanzee, and before that, a line of species going back to microorganisms that lived in the ocean? God may have "simply" kick-started evolution to eventually produce man, which he then imbued with His likeness.

Does this theistic evolution violate the biblical story of creation? I believe it only does if too literal a view is taken of the Genesis accounts. But those accounts can, and should, be read as Hebrew poetry.

11

Is the Bible True?

"The Bible is not the 'word of God', but stolen from pagan sources. Its Eden, Adam and Eve were taken from the Babylonian accounts; its Flood and Deluge is but an epitome of some four hundred flood accounts; its Ark and Ararat have their equivalents in a score of Deluge myths; even the names of Noah's sons are copies, so also Isaac's sacrifice, Solomon's judgment, and Samson's pillar acts; its Moses is fashioned after the Syrian Mises; its laws after Hammurabi's code. Its Messiah is derived from the Egyptian Mahdi, Savior, certain verses are verbatim copies of Egyptian scriptures. Between Jesus and the Egyptian Horus, Gerald Massy found 137 similarities, and those between Christ and Krishna run into the hundreds. How then can the Bible be a revelation to the Jews?"
-- Lloyd Graham, Deceptions and Myths of the Bible

"No archeological discovery has ever controverted a Biblical reference. Scores of archeological findings have been made which confirm in clear outline or in exact detail historical statements in the Bible. And, by the same token, proper evaluation of Biblical descriptions has often led to amazing discoveries."
-- Dr. Nelson Glueck, authority on Israeli archeology

There are many questions on the Bible that Cliffe is challenged on. Some have to do with the reliability of the Biblical texts. Others have to do with apparent contradictions in the text. And still others have to do with issues such as the authorship of the individual books of the Bible, or their divine inspiration.

In addressing the reliability of the New Testament books, Cliffe says "The New Testament that we have today is based on over five thousand two hundred Greek manuscripts or pieces of manuscript dated from the 1st through the 10th century AD found from Rome, Italy, down around the Mediterranean to Alexandria, Egypt, all agreeing to an infinitesimal degree."

A common apologetics argument is to compare the number of ancient manuscripts we have for the New Testament versus the number we have for other ancient documents, as well as comparing the gap in time between the manuscripts and the original source document. Google 'New Testament manuscript evidence' to get a slew of websites which provide this evidence, many with charts for easy comparison. The ancient document which comes closest to the New Testament in quantity of manuscripts and chronological proximity to the original is Homer's Iliad, and it comes in a distant second place.

One question that pops up is about the apparent difference between the Old and New Testaments as far as God's demeanor and behavior are concerned. The Old Testament seems to portray a wrathful and vengeful God, whereas the New Testament shows God to be merciful and long-suffering.

Cliffe has responded to this question by asking the student crowd which is the bloodiest book in the Bible. One might think it could be the book of Exodus, where God kills the firstborn of the children of Egypt, or perhaps Deuteronomy, where God has His people, the Israelites, kill entire peoples. Or Genesis, where God brings a global flood to drown almost all the people of the earth. But Cliffe points out that it is rather the Book of Revelation, the last book in the New Testament, which is the bloodiest, where locusts with teeth like lions' teeth are sent to torture mankind for five months[60], or where angels are released to kill a third of mankind.[61]

---

[60] Revelation 9:10.

Some students object to the Bible and the Resurrection by saying that the Gospel accounts record the event differently. For instance, in Matthew, only one angel is mentioned at the empty tomb[62]. But in Luke, two angels are mentioned[63]. Matthew mentions two women arriving at the empty tomb, whereas John only mentions one[64]. There are many other differences in the accounts. At first thought, this might seem to be damning evidence against the veracity of the Resurrection story. But Cliffe astutely points out that these differences are actually good to have. If the accounts agreed totally, then that would point to collusion or one writer copying another. Also, if the differences contradicted each other, that would be a fatal problem. For example, if Matthew said that there was **only** one angel at the tomb, then that would contradict what Luke testified to. But the Resurrection accounts do not contain any logical contradictions. So having mostly common details, while having some divergent details, as long as they are not contradictory, point to independent witnesses telling the story as they saw it or remembered it.

Although there are difficult passages in the Bible, Cliffe reminds students of what Mark Twain once said: "It ain't those parts of the Bible that I can't understand that bother me, it is the parts that I do understand."[65]

Occasionally, questions about how the Bible treats slavery come up. There are many verses that seem to condone

---

[61] Revelation 9:15.
[62] Matthew 28:2-7.
[63] Luke 24:2-7.
[64] John 20:1-18.
[65]

http://quotations.about.com/od/marktwainquotes/a/twainreligion.htm

slavery. A particularly horrific one is Exodus 21:20-21, which says "Anyone who beats their male or female slave with a rod must be punished if the slave dies as a direct result, but they are not to be punished if the slave recovers after a day or two, since the slave is their property."[66] What? They are not to be punished if the slave recovers after a couple days? Do you realize how bad the beating must be in order to not recover until two days later? That's just horrible. My faith takes a dip just reading verses like that.

The argument is made though that God is not interested as much in correcting societal ills as He is in showing man's need for salvation. When we only think of this life on earth, we feel that what's all-important is justice in this life, comfort in this life, freedom in this life. But God repeatedly points out in the Bible that this life is fleeting and what we should keep our minds and hearts fixed on is the eternal life hereafter. As James writes: "You are just a vapor that appears for a little while and then vanishes away."[67]

---

[66] NIV.
[67] From James 4:14, NIV.

12

Other Open-Air Preachers

Tom Short

Pastor Tom Short is also an experienced national open-air campus evangelist. A few years younger than Cliffe, Short was born on March 23, 1957. He lives in Columbus, Ohio with his wife and five children and spends a good portion of the year doing open-air apologetics and evangelism at college campuses, similar to what Cliffe does. He has visited over 100 college campuses over the years, beginning even before Cliffe, in the late 70s. I first became aware of him when I drove up two hours from Tampa Bay in October 2002 to see Cliffe at the University of Florida in Gainesville. Cliffe was speaking in Turlington Plaza, a central area on campus where large numbers of students pass through on their way between classes. I heard another middle-aged man preaching loudly nearby, so I walked over to listen. This was Pastor Tom. He seemed more extreme than Cliffe, more "fire and brimstone".

Years later, in 2010 or 2011, I caught him at UT Austin. He was preaching at the end of the West Mall because he wasn't officially invited by a student organization, so he couldn't preach closer to the UT Tower.

He was attempting to initiate conversations with student passersby by showing them a series of posterboards of famous or infamous men in history. One was of Adolf Hitler, another was of Charles Darwin, and there were others. He asked a student whom he caught the attention of a simple question: "Was this a good man?" while displaying the posterboard of Adolf Hitler. The student would of course inevitably answer in the negative. Then he would show other people whose goodness or evil were clear. Finally, he would pull out the posterboard of Charles Darwin's face and ask if the student thought he was good or evil. The student would usually say that Darwin was good, or at least not evil. Tom would then begin a lengthy explanation of how he feels that Darwin's ideas are responsible for perhaps more evil than anyone else in history, because they opened the door wide open to secularism and then atheism.

He lately appears on campuses with large attractive, full-color banners that he puts up for passing students to read. They deal with various topics, including evidence for God's existence, creation vs. evolution, the evidence for Jesus's deity and resurrection, arguments against atheism and secularism, and other topics. He enlists the assistance of interns who travel with him. He has an active Facebook page and Twitter account. His ministry's website is tomthepreacher.com. In 2001 he wrote a book, '5 Crucial Questions About Christianity', with an updated cover and a companion website, 5crucialquestions.com.

Brother Jed

George Edward Smock, known on college campuses as Brother Jed, is another busy open-air evangelist. Born in 1943, Brother Jed is an extreme "fire and brimstone" preacher who enjoys being provocative and saying shocking things which offend many students who stop to listen to him. His ministry's busy website is www.brojed.org. Perusing it one can see many of the harsh things he says and does. He calls many students "children of the Devil" and draws ire from the gay and lesbian groups on the campuses he visits. I have never had the experience of seeing him preach, but it seems from the long weekly email reports I receive that his appearance on campus is as much circus as it is serious discussion.

Max Lynch

Then there's the late Max Lynch. Max was once a professor of mathematics at Indiana State University. I saw him a few times also out on the U of I quad in the early 90s. He would wear casual business clothes, topped off with a baseball cap, which didn't look quite right. He would preach rather loudly, basically shouting, emphatically shaking a Bible he had in one of his hands. He would mostly rail against all sins sexual, from fornication and homosexuality to lust and pornography. Every so often, to lubricate his throat after shouting for several minutes, he would walk over to the large tree he was preaching near and grab a clear plastic or glass container holding what looked like orange juice. Hecklers watching would then take this opportunity to yell out "Screwdriver!", implying that the drink contained more than merely orange juice. Max wasn't phased. After taking a couple gulps of the juice, he would set the bottle back down and continue preaching.

One story Max would tell was shocking though. He would mention that his wife would occasionally disobey or speak up against him at their home. With his arm lifted, swinging his Bible around, Max would tell the students that at those times he would "hit her with the truth of God", clearly indicating that this was a literal hit using his Bible and not just a figurative one. Needless to say, the students watching this story retold were aghast.

I was impressed though by Max's conviction for Christ in one story I read about him on Brother Jed's website[68]. The story goes that in October 1976, on the eve of the presidential election, Democratic candidate Jimmy Carter was about to speak outside at Southern Illinois University. Before the motorcade arrived, Max climbed a tree where the crowd was gathered awaiting Mr. Carter. When Carter arrived and began to speak, Max yelled out from his high perch "Repent!" When Carter began speaking about what he had planned to discuss, inflation and unemployment, Max yelled from above "What about abortion? What about the rising crime rate? What about drunkenness and dope addiction? What about divorce?" and other social and moral ills. Now Jimmy Carter had publicly professed during his candidacy that he was a born-again Christian, and yet, according to Brother Jed's story, he didn't address Max's concerns about people's sins. Instead, he just got frustrated and cut short his speech. This story raises my respect for Max Lynch, and lowers my respect a bit for Jimmy Carter.

Others

I remember one afternoon on the U of I quad when Cliffe was doing his thing when this guy comes over toward Cliffe lugging a 7-foot wooden cross. He interrupts Cliffe and tells the crowd of students that Cliffe is preaching a weak message that isn't the gospel at all - that what Cliffe was actually doing was leading the students off to hell instead of heaven. I remember thinking that this is what happens in the Bible Belt (although central Illinois is perhaps just north of the northern edge of what's considered the Bible Belt)!

---

[68] http://www.brojed.org/maxlynch.php

Another time on the Quad I saw a guy with his 3 young children lined up stoically beside him. He was preaching a very conservative "old-time religion" message and would frequently point to one of his children and shout out a Bible book name and chapter number, to which that child would then immediately rattle off the entire chapter from memory. It was impressive but also a little sad and spooky. The children didn't look happy.

A Word About Campuses Visited

Cliffe, like all the other national campus evangelists I am aware of, overwhelmingly visits campuses outside of areas that are generally considered liberal. Where do you think of when you think of places and universities which have a liberal bent? I think of the Northeast, including New York State, Massachusetts, New Jersey, Pennsylvania, etc. I also think of California and the Northwest. These are heavily-populated states where Cliffe and other evangelists spend little or no time in. I believe Cliffe primarily speaks in Texas, Arizona, Colorado, and Florida. Pastor Tom Short mainly stays in the Midwest, going to universities in Ohio, Indiana, Illinois, Iowa, etc. This is disappointing because they are not often going where the need to hear the Good News is arguably the greatest. In Luke 10:2, Jesus says "The harvest is plentiful, but the workers are few." These preachers are some of the few workers, however more workers are needed where the harvest is most plentiful: the Northeast, California, and the Northwest.

Why do these evangelists not visit the areas of the country where they are needed the most? There are many reasons. The primary reason is that the Christian student organizations in these Bible Belt universities are more numerous, larger, and perhaps more aggressive in their desire to introduce people to

Christ and Christianity. Cliffe and his fellow evangelists need to be sponsored by one of these groups in order to help defray the financial cost of a visit. Cliffe also has a long relationship with some of these universities and visits them each year, often at around the same time. For example, at the University of Texas at Austin, Cliffe returns there each November as a personal houseguest of Greg Grooms of The Hill House, a Christian study center near the University modeled in part on L'Abri Fellowship, begun in Switzerland in 1955 by the late great Christian theologian and philosopher Francis Schaeffer.

13

Miscellaneous

I occasionally post to a blog at www.cliffeknechtle.com. There I post my comments about things I've heard Cliffe say. Some things Cliffe says I agree with, some other things I take issue with.

I've watched Cliffe speak perhaps on a couple dozen afternoons, mostly in the early 1990s at the University of Illinois at Urbana-Champaign, but also on a few days in 2002 at the University of Florida in Gainesville and in 2010 at the University of Texas at Austin[69]. He always attracts more men than he does women - I would say the ratio is about 2 to 1. Why is that? I believe it's because men are generally more interested in apologetics than women. Men are generally more impassioned by arguments relating to ideas and logic, whereas women are generally more attuned to emotional reasoning. Both are valid ways of finding truth, but the former is what Cliffe specializes in.

And as for the students who stand up to engage Cliffe with a question, the ratio is even more lopsided. I would say the questioners are 80% to even 90% male. You can verify this by watching one of the dozens of YouTube videos from Cliffe's campus outdoor sessions. I believe the reason for this, besides the fact that men are more interested in apologetics and argumentation, is that men are less likely to

---

[69] See http://www.worldmag.com/2013/05/real_commencement regarding Cliffe's apologetics ministry, including a photo I took of him at UT Austin in 2010.

be fearful to stand up and speak in front of a group of their peers.

Why does Cliffe do what he does? Is he trying to help win souls for Christ? Certainly. Does he enjoy the intellectual apologetic banter? Of course. Is he looking for new material for his TV show? Yes. But what is the reason Cliffe gives for doing what he does? He says his aim is to introduce people to his greatest friend: Jesus Christ.

Cliffe has said on several occasions that "the only reason an atheist doesn't find God is the same reason a thief doesn't find a policeman – he's running away". Is there merit to this assertion? For some atheists, I believe there is. For those unbelievers, they have been enjoying a life unfettered by the restraining dictates of a God they see as someone who crimps their style. They have embraced "the world" and all the pleasures it offers, and have no desire to temper their fun by following a God who requires self-sacrifice and obedience.

In Cliffe's YouTube Give Me An Answer episode #2812, a student assumes that Cliffe is Christian because his parents probably were. Cliffe was extremely offended by this assumption. He eventually admits that the student's assumption is correct, but Cliffe is still offended that the student doesn't think he came to faith in Christ through his own study and searching. But that student made a good point that seemed to have escaped Cliffe's understanding. It **is** true that it is a statistical probability that people adhere to the faith of their parents. How many children in Afghanistan grow up to believe in any religion other than Islam? A very small percentage. How many children in Italy grow up to be anything other than a Roman Catholic? A small percentage. Where you are born has a huge effect on the typical person as to what God he or she believes in. That is a disturbing truth, because if Christianity is true and if one must confess Jesus Christ as one's Lord and Savior, then just being born in a non-Christian country, which most people on Earth are, means that one has little chance of being saved and avoiding hell.

I don't believe God works this way. I don't believe one needs to actually confess the name of Jesus Christ in order to be saved. If He did require this, then how could He also be considered a good God, knowing that most people ever born would either not know of Jesus's name, or even if they heard of Jesus sometime during their lifetime, would not be taught the Gospel message, or come to understand the Gospel message.

Some may bring up here the verses I mentioned in the chapter on hell, John 14:6 ("I am the way and the truth and the life. No one comes to the Father except through me") and Acts 4:12 ("there is no other name under heaven given to mankind by which we must be saved"). But neither of these verses demand that the individual actually name Jesus as their personal Savior. They can merely mean that Jesus is the means of salvation – that the Father accepts us through the work of Jesus, not that a vocal or mental pronouncement of the word 'Jesus' or 'Yeshua' or the like is required, nor even do they necessarily mean that one must acknowledge that it was Jesus who provided the means for their forgiveness before God. These verses may simply mean that, in God's eyes, it is the redeeming work of His son which provided the basis for the salvation of all those who will escape God's wrath.

There is also an objection to belief in God put forth by the 18th-century French philosopher Voltaire. He famously said that "those who can make you believe absurdities can make you commit atrocities."[70] There certainly have been many heinous acts throughout history committed by people who

---

[70] http://en.wikiquote.org/wiki/Voltaire

have believed some demonstrably false beliefs in supreme beings, who were emboldened to commit such acts because of those very beliefs. This is the major theme in the late great atheist Christopher Hitchens' book 'God Is Not Great: How Religion Poisons Everything'[71].

Over the years, several students listening to Cliffe think that he bashes atheists, that he believes that atheists can't be good people. But he rightfully points out that he says or believes no such thing. He mentions that some of his best friends are atheists, and that they are very altruistic, that they love their wives and children, and that they even care for the downtrodden. His issue with them is that they cannot consistently live out their atheism. They cannot live as if anything goes, that any bad behavior, no matter how cruel, is morally as acceptable as good behavior.

One question which I have heard asked is how can Christians fully enjoy heaven if someone they love is spending eternity in hell. This is a good question. Most saved Christians have loved ones that aren't saved and will not become saved. If these people end up in hell, how can a Christian be entirely happy in heaven knowing that they have loved ones spending eternity in a place of misery? Revelation 21:4 says that God "will wipe every tear from their eyes. There will be no more death or mourning or crying or pain". So either God automatically removes the sad thoughts we have of our loved ones agonizing in hell or He enlightens us as to why we should not be mourning for their suffering. Frankly, either alternative is unpalatable.

Students sometimes object that God doesn't exist because they pray for things and God doesn't grant their wishes. Cliffe has responded that the point of prayer is to develop a

---

[71] published by Twelve, 336 pages, 2009.

relationship with God, not to get things from him. God isn't some magic genie that we ask wishes from.

Cliffe has said that we draw to God because of a hatred of loneliness. I agree. When one feels truly alone in this world, that is such a depressing and terrifying feeling that one reaches out to God for companionship.

In the Give Me An Answer YouTube video #1810, at Ohio State, you can easily overhear one student in the background say "This guy's good … he's good. I don't like him, but he's good." I love this random comment. It shows a student who respects Cliffe's knowledge, speaking ability, and the quality of his arguments, yet at the same time, he admits that he doesn't like Cliffe, which to me seems that he is admitting that he doesn't wish to change his life even if Christianity is true.

Cliffe mentions the story of his younger brother Stuart who said would spend hours answering the challenges from his atheist or agnostic dormmates at Princeton. Stuart would eventually tell his friends that he would pull an all-nighter if his dormmates had true intellectual problems that were keeping them from putting their faith in Christ. But if the real issue for them was that they didn't want to follow God because that would mean that they would have to change their lifestyles - that they would have to stop sleeping around or stop cheating on exams so they could get into the best medical schools – then Stuart said let's stop kidding ourselves. Without fail, his dormmates would admit that they weren't really stymied by intellectual doubts.

14

Why I Wrote This Book

Listening to and participating in some of Cliffe's campus visits over the past two decades has been one of the great joys of my adult life. I truly love philosophical discussions and debates, especially those that involve the most important questions of life. Chief of those questions is whether God exists or not. My interest in these discussions probably began in 1985 when I was a freshman at Rensselaer Polytechnic Institute in upstate New York. My fellow dormmates (all male) were very bright, many of them high school valedictorians or with perfect SAT math scores. Late at night, while devouring $4 large pizzas from one of a large number of local pizza joints, we would often get into deep philosophical discussions. The most interesting and heated ones dealt with religion or God's existence. After all, is there any question more important than whether or not God exists?

When I began my graduate studies at UIUC in 1991, I was still a Catholic, although my faith wasn't something I focused a lot of time on. But Protestant Christianity was very prominent on the Illinois campus, and there were some student groups and local pastors who were brazenly hostile to Catholicism. I was initially offended by these "Catholic haters". I remember one afternoon while sitting on a concrete ledge just outside the student union having my lunch, looking up at a tree branch about five feet above my head and noticing a tiny booklet taped to the branch. I pulled this booklet off the branch and noticed it was a comic book. I thought "what's this?" and began to read it. I quickly realized this was no childish comic book. It was a very extreme Christian fundamentalist religious tract. It was a "Chick tract", published by Chick Publications which was founded by comic artist Jack Chick more than 50 years ago. Its purpose was to use the fear of unending torment in hell to convince the reader that he/she should put their faith in Jesus Christ and become a Christian.

I came to find out that these tracts were placed by student members of a local fundamentalist church. When one afternoon I noticed that that church had set up a long table on the U of I quad to pass out Chick tracts, I promptly darted over to the table to take a closer look. There I noticed that there were a few virulently anti-Catholic tracts. One of them was entitled 'Are Roman Catholics Christians?' I asked the pastor about these, and he defended them. This incensed me, so I got "in his grill". We were speaking just inches away from each other. He accused me of being full of pride. But I didn't back down. Eventually, I left and walked back to the student union close by. When I was just halfway down the hallway, a student ran up to me. He told me he was from the table with the tracts and he wanted to apologize for the behavior of his pastor. He said I had instead hurt his pastor's pride and that he was just arguing with me as a way of protecting his flock.

Back then, in my early 20s, I may have been a bit proud. I perhaps wanted to prove too much that I was right, and thereby prove that some others were wrong. But, even then, and ever since then, the overwhelming reason I am so interested in apologetics is because I want to know the truth. I so badly want to know for certain whether God exists or not. I don't want to just have faith that He exists, no matter how strong that faith may be at times. I want to KNOW whether He truly exists. In this lifelong quest, I aim to be as honest as possible. If I ever find the truth intellectually, I will embrace it. I will not ignore it if I happen at the time to wish the truth to be something else.

I obviously have many questions. Questions about the truth, questions about God, questions about Christianity, etc. I hope I don't ever come across as irreverent. That is never my intention. I would never wish to insult God in any way. I believe though that God welcomes the questions, the frustrations, even sometimes the anger of His creations. As long as a heart is searching, I don't believe there is any danger of offending a loving God.

Faith is clearly a struggle for me. Many mornings I wake up feeling that God doesn't exist. And it's more than just my feelings. It's also the intellectual doubts which plague me. I have studied theology and apologetics for over 20 years now, but I have found few answers to the big questions. That could be expected however, since lay people and theologians have wrestled with the big questions about God and Christianity for thousands of years, and still the questions remain.

And yet I hold dearly to the hope that God exists. There have been a few remarkable moments in my life where I felt that God intervened and answered an urgent prayer or showed His presence by way of a very unlikely event. So there are several reasons why I wanted to write this book. Besides my love of apologetics and my quest for the most important answers in life, I wanted to write about the ministry of Cliffe Knechtle which has had such a big impact on my spiritual education and journey[72]. I wanted also to

---

[72] In writing this book, I wondered whether I should reach out to Cliffe for a personal interview. I decided against it for a number of reasons. One of them was that his ministry did not seem to want

discuss the main topics he raises and give my input on the merits or weaknesses of each of his arguments, and to point out that the issues discussed are often much more complex and nuanced than they first seem. And I definitely wanted to introduce more college students to Cliffe so they can hopefully go see him speak on their campus (or a nearby one), learn more about him, acquire his books, research his ministry, and most of all, study the subject matter and come to either faith in Jesus Christ or, if they honestly come to believe that Jesus is not the Son of God, then at least they will have arrived at that conclusion by an honest study of the evidence.

---

to speak with me about my book. The administrative head of Cliffe's Give Me An Answer ministry reached out to me once, letting me know that he knew that I was writing a book about Cliffe, and that he wanted to chat with me about it. I enthusiastically agreed, but then he went silent. I suggested some times to talk, but I was ignored. I still followed up once or twice, but received no response. Evidently, he or Cliffe changed their mind and decided not to talk to me about my book. I found, and still do find, that rather odd.

Appendix A

Cliffe's Books

Give Me An Answer That Satisfies My Heart & My Mind, IVP (InterVarsity Press) Books, 1986, ISBN-13 978-0877845690, 165 pp.

Cliffe's first book, it deals with a lot of top questions in a very readable way. It has many humorous drawings illustrating various theological points.

Help Me Believe: Direct Answers to Real Questions, IVP Books, 2000, ISBN-13 978-0830822683, 131 pp.

Cliffe's second book is similar to his first in that it answers common questions asked of him, although the questions addressed in this book are generally not as commonly asked as the ones in 'Give Me An Answer'.

Heaven Can't Wait, Business Books International, 2005, ISBN-13 978-0916673215, 304 pp.

This is an edited collection of several of Cliffe's sermons over the years.

Faithful Witness: The Urbana 84 Compendium, IVP, edited by James McLeish, 1985, 200 pp., p.18-25.

Urbana[73] is the largest student missions conference in the world. Began in 1957 with Billy Graham as the keynote speaker, Urbana is held every 3 years in Urbana, Illinois, home to the University of Illinois at Urbana-Champaign, which has one of the largest numbers of students in Christian organizations such as InterVarsity Christian Fellowship and Campus Crusade For Christ. On the first day of the Urbana 84 conference, Cliffe gave a talk entitled 'Testimony of Faithfulness to the Great Commission', which is chapter 2 in the book.

---

[73] https://urbana.org

Appendix B

Give Me An Answer Television Program

The Give Me An Answer television program debuted in 1991 on Connecticut TV. It airs Sunday mornings on WTNH, channel 8 for Connecticut viewers.

The show centers around Cliffe's campus trips. In the half-hour program, an edited clip from a university is shown, featuring students asking questions at a microphone, after which Cliffe provides his answer. After about 20 minutes of this Q&A, Cliffe appears by himself for about 5 minutes to give a little mini-sermon. Finally, he concludes by inviting the viewer to attend his church where he is the senior pastor, Grace Community Church in New Canaan, Connecticut.

Appendix C

Cliffe's Online Debates

This is a list of some of Cliffe's public debates.

Debate Title: The Great Debate: Atheism vs. Christianity
Opponent: Michael Newdow
Date: December 8, 2002
Location: Rolling Hills Christian Church, Sacramento, California

This debate was sponsored by the Church Communications Network (CCN) and was broadcast to over 1,500 churches and other sites, and was watched by over 250,000 people.

Michael Newdow is an atheist infamous for suing in 2002 to remove the phrase "under God" from the Pledge of Allegiance.

Debate Title: Is Christianity Rational?
Opponent: Jeremy Beahan of Reasonable Doubts (doubtcast.org)
Date: October 7, 2010
Location: Michigan State University, East Lansing, Michigan

From the Facebook page on the event:

Jeremy Beahan is the Producer & Co-host of the Reasonable Doubts Podcast and radio show which provides a skeptical guide to religion with a focus on counter-apologetics. Jeremy teaches college classes in Philosophy, World Religions, Biblical Literature, Aesthetics, and Critical Thinking at Kendall College of Art and Design/Ferris State University.

Fundamentalist raised and educated, Jeremy graduated from Grace Bible College and Cornerstone University with a dual degree in social studies and religious education. While training for ministry Jeremy underwent a dramatic de-conversion as a culmination to many years of questioning. Today Jeremy works to promote critical thinking and skeptical inquiry in his local community - he has been an active member of the Freethought Association (now CFI Michigan) since 2002.

Debate Title: Is Belief In The Christian God Rational?
Opponent: Matt Dillahunty of The Atheist Experience
Date: November 26, 2012
Location: Texas State University, San Marcos, Texas

Matt Dillahunty is an atheist speaker and was the president of the Atheist Community of Austin from 2006 to 2013. He hosts the cable-access TV show The Atheist Experience and is the founder of the counter-apologetics encyclopedia Iron Chariots (wiki.ironchariots.org).

Debate Title: Does God Exist?
Opponent: Matt Dillahunty of The Atheist Experience
Date: October 3, 2013
Location: Texas State University, San Marcos, Texas

Cliffe has also debated the famous atheist Madalyn Murray O'Hair about 20 years ago, as well as Bart Ehrman at UNC-Chapel Hill circa 1991.

Appendix D

Some Campuses Which Cliffe Regularly Visits

University of Illinois at Urbana-Champaign
uiuc.edu

My alma mater; Cliffe has visited UIUC many times over the past 20 or 30 years; he has often been a guest of UIUC's InterVarsity chapter, which is one of the very largest in the nation.

YouTube video numbers: #2108, #1008 (e.g.: to find video #2108, on youtube.com, search for 'give me an answer 2108')

University of Texas at Austin
utaustin.edu

Cliffe has visited UT Austin many times over the years. He often visits in November before Thanksgiving. There are many, many YouTube videos of Cliffe's sessions at UT Austin, far more than any other school.

UT Austin is also the home of the Hill House, a Christian study center located near campus. See hillhouseaustin.org. When Cliffe visits UT Austin each November, he stays at the Hill House as a personal houseguest of Greg's.

From his November 2013 visit: #0114, #0214, #0314, #0514, #0614, #0714, #0814, #0914, #1014, #1114, #1214, #1314

From his November 2012 visit: #0213, #0313, #0413, #0613, #0713, #1113, #1213, #1313, #1413, #1513, #2013, #2113, #2213, #2613, #2713, #3313

From his November 2011 visit: #0112, #0212, #0312, #0412, #0512, #0612, #0712, #0812, #0912, #1012, #1112, #1212, #1312, #1412, #1512, #1612, #1712, #1812, #2212, #2312, #2412, #2512, #2712, #2812, #2912

From his November 2010 visit: #0111, #0211, #0711, #0811, #0911, #1311, #1411, #1511, #1611, #1711, #2011, #2111, #2211, #2311, #2411, #2511, #2611, #2711, #2811, #2911, #3011, #3111, #3211

From his November 2009 visit: #1510, #1710, #2310, #2410, #2510, #2610, #2710, #3010, #3110, #3210

From his November 2008 visit: #1409, #1509, #2609

University of Florida at Gainesville
uf.edu

I saw Cliffe at UF in October 2002; Pastor Tom Short coincidentally happened to be there the same week. Cliffe had videos of this visit on his website (givemeananswer.org) for years, some with me in them, but they have since all been removed.

University of Arizona
arizona.edu

Cliffe's YouTube videos taped at the U of Arizona:

October 2008 – #0109, #0209, #0609, #2009

October 2009 – #1110, #2010, #2110
October 2010 – #0511, #0611, #1811, #1911, #2810, #2910
October 2012 – #2112, #0113, #0813, #0913, #1013, #1813, #1913, #2813, #2913, #0414

Northern Illinois University
niu.edu

October 2012 - #1912, #2012, #3012, #3112

Texas State University
txstate.edu

November 2012 - #2612, #3212, #0513, #1613, #1713
October 2013 - #2313, #2413, #2513, #3013, #3113, #3213

Ohio State University
osu.edu

May 2010 – #0610, #0710, #0810, #1610, #1810, #2210, #0311, #0411, #1011, #1111, #1211

Michigan State University
msu.edu

September 2009 – #1709, #1809, #2709, #2809, #2909, #0910, #1010

University of Maine
umaine.edu

Harvard University harvard.edu	
MIT mit.edu	
University of Wisconsin – Madison wisc.edu	
University of Minnesota umn.edu	
University of California Los Angeles ucla.edu	
University of California San Diego ucsd.edu	
University of California Santa Barbara ucsb.edu	
University of California Berkeley berkeley.edu	
Stanford University stanford.edu	

University of Rhode Island
uri.edu

University of Connecticut
uconn.edu

April 2009 - #1310,2209,1410,2409,1910,2309,2109

Columbia University
columbia.edu

University of Virginia
virginia.edu

University of North Carolina at Chapel Hill
unc.edu

University of Georgia
uga.edu

University of Michigan at Ann Arbor
umich.edu

Duke University
duke.edu

North Carolina State University
ncsu.edu

Florida State University
fsu.edu

Appendix E

Student Organizations Sponsoring Cliffe

The following are some campus student organizations that have sponsored Cliffe's visits:

InterVarsity Christian Fellowship (IVCF)
intervarsity.org

InterVarsity is an inter-denominational Christian ministry founded in 1941 and is now on over 600 college and university campuses in the United States. More than 40,000 students and faculty participate in IVCF. Their publishing arm, InterVarsity Press (ivpress.com), publishes over 100 new books each year. Every three years, up to 20,000 students attend Urbana, their student mission conference.

I first saw Cliffe because in the early 1990s IVCF sponsored his visits to the University of Illinois at Urbana-Champaign, where I was a graduate student.

Campus Crusade for Christ (CCC)
cru.org

Campus Crusade for Christ (aka Cru; I knew it in college as Campus Crusade or "C Cubed") is an interdenominational evangelical Christian organization founded in 1951 at UCLA by Bill Bright. In 1991 it moved its headquarters to Orlando, and in 2011 the US chapter changed its name to just Cru.

They are famous for their booklet The Four Spiritual Laws, authored by Bill Bright in 1952.

Beta Upsilon Chi (BYX, "Bucks", Brothers Under Christ)
betaupsilonchi.org

Beta Upsilon Chi is a Christian fraternity formed at UT Austin in 1985. They are now in 34 campuses in 15 states. They have sponsored Cliffe for his November visits to UT Austin.

Hill House
hillhouseaustin.org

Hill House is a Christian study center located near the campus of the University of Texas at Austin. Formerly the ProbeCenter, it was founded in 1989 and modeled in part on L'Abri Fellowship, begun in Switzerland in 1955 by the late great Christian theologian and philosopher Francis Schaeffer. It has been headed since 1994 by Greg Grooms, who had worked with L'Abri for 15 years.

When Cliffe visits UT Austin each November, he stays at the Hill House as a personal houseguest of Mr. Grooms.

Made in the USA
Middletown, DE
30 January 2016